Cambridge Industrial and Commercial Series

General Editor: G. F. BOSWORTH, F.R.G.S.

TRADE AND COMMERCE

TRADE AND COMMERCE

WITH SOME ACCOUNT OF OUR COINAGE,
WEIGHTS AND MEASURES, BANKS
AND EXCHANGES

by

A. J. DICKS, B.A., B.Sc.

Cambridge :
at the University Press
1915

CAMBRIDGE UNIVERSITY PRESS
Cambridge, New York, Melbourne, Madrid, Cape Town,
Singapore, São Paulo, Delhi, Mexico City

Cambridge University Press
The Edinburgh Building, Cambridge CB2 8RU, UK

Published in the United States of America by Cambridge University Press, New York

www.cambridge.org
Information on this title: www.cambridge.org/9781107640924

First published 1915
First paperback edition 2013

A catalogue record for this publication is available from the British Library

ISBN 978-1-107-64092-4 Paperback

GENERAL PREFACE

THE books in this Series deal with the industrial and commercial condition of our country. Of the importance of the subject there can be no doubt, for it is the story of the material side of the life of a great nation. British agriculture is the most enterprising in the world; British manufactures, both textile and hardware, are famed in all parts of the globe; British ships are on every sea and carry for other nations as well as for ourselves; and Britain, through the Banks and Exchanges of London, is the centre of the money market of the world.

It has been well said that material needs cannot be neglected or forgotten with impunity in this world. Just as a man must have bread to eat if he wishes to enjoy life, so a nation needs material prosperity if it is to be of real influence in the world. Industrial and commercial prosperity does not, in itself, constitute greatness, but it is a condition without which national greatness is impossible. Hence, the story of the industrial and commercial condition of Britain is worth telling to our school children, not only that they may rejoice in our country's progress, but, also, that they may realise the responsibilities borne by the citizens of the first of all nations.

G. F. B.

EDITOR'S NOTE

THIS book is of great importance in this series for it deals with the Trade and Commerce of Britain. Our Weights and Measures and our Coinage are historically considered and then contrasted with the Metric and Monetary Systems of the Continent. Then follows some account of the work of the Royal Mint, while the Post Office with its many branches of activity receives a good deal of attention. Our Food Supply and our Foreign and Colonial Markets, together with the work of our great Banks, Exchanges, and the Custom House are carefully treated: and such difficult subjects as Foreign Exchange, Bill Broking, our Bullion and Gold Reserve are explained so that much of our recent financial history is made clear to the young reader. There are also chapters detailing the work of the Board of Trade and the Patent Office, describing the formation and business of Joint Stock Companies, and explaining the meaning of Under-writing at "Lloyds'."

Teachers and Students who wish to study in greater detail any part of the Industrial and Commercial History are advised to use Dr Cunningham's *Growth of English Industry and Commerce*, published by the Cambridge University Press. There they will find full and accurate references to a large number of authorities in all branches of this subject.

G. F. B.

August, 1915

CONTENTS

CHAP.   PAGE

1.   ENGLISH WEIGHTS AND MEASURES   1

2.   THE METRIC SYSTEM   7

3.   ENGLISH COINS AND THEIR HISTORY   10

4.   OTHER MONETARY SYSTEMS   15

5.   THE ROYAL MINT AND ITS WORK   19

6.   THE POST OFFICE AND ITS WORK   25

7.   OUR FOOD AND ITS SOURCES OF SUPPLY   .   .   .   29

8.   THE IMPORTS OF THE UNITED KINGDOM   .   .   .   37

9.   EXPORTS AND FOREIGN MARKETS   42

10. OUR CONSULS AND THEIR WORK IN FOREIGN LANDS .   45

11. BANKS AND BANKING   48

12. THE BANK OF ENGLAND   52

13. THE CLEARING HOUSE   57

14. EXCHANGES AND THE MONEY MARKET   .   .   .   60

15. BULLION AND GOLD RESERVES   65

16. THE EXCHANGES OF LONDON   67

17. THE BOARD OF TRADE   72

18. TRADE MARKS   74

19. PATENTS   77

20. LIMITED LIABILITY COMPANIES   80

21. UNDERWRITING   84

22. THE CUSTOMS AND EXCISE   89

     INDEX   93

ILLUSTRATIONS

PAGE

Old English Standards 6

Gold noble of Edward III 11

Swiss 20 franc piece; French 2 franc and 20 franc pieces 16

German 20 mark piece 17

Goldsmiths' Hall: the Grand Staircase (*Phot.* A. Bridgen) 21

The General Post Office (*Phot.* Frith) 26

Loading grain from an elevator 30

Freezing mutton, New Zealand 32

Butter-making, New Zealand 33

An Australian vineyard 35

Drying fruit in Australia 36

Sawing timber with steam-saw, Western Australia . . 39

Skins drying, New South Wales 40

Facsimile of a cheque 49

The Bank of England and the Royal Exchange (*Phot.*
    Valentine) 53

Wool store, Adelaide 70

Somerset House (*Phot.* Frith) 81

Lloyd's: The Casualty Board and Register . . . 85

The Custom House (*Phot.* Frith) 90

The illustrations on pp. 6, 11, 16, 17 are from the *Encyclopaedia Britannica* (11th edition); those on pp. 32 and 33 are from photographs kindly supplied by the Government of New Zealand; those on pp. 36, 39, 40, 70 from photographs supplied by the Commonwealth of Australia; that on p. 30 from a photograph supplied by the Canadian Government; that on p. 35 from a photograph supplied by Messrs Burgoyne; that on p. 85 from a block lent by Messrs André Sleigh and Anglo, Ltd.; that on p. 49 is reproduced by courtesy of Messrs Barclay and Co., Ltd.

1. ENGLISH WEIGHTS AND MEASURES

Two systems of weights and measures are recognised in the United Kingdom at the present time: the Imperial system and the Metric system. The Imperial system is the one with which we are all familiar, and which has the yard, pound, and gallon as units of length, weight, and capacity respectively. The Metric system is a more recent system introduced from France; its units of length, weight, and capacity are the metre, kilogram, and litre. As the Imperial system is somewhat cumbrous and difficult, it will be a matter of interest to consider its origin and development.

The earliest units of linear measurement used by ancient nations undoubtedly arose from measurements of parts of the human body; thus we may recall that the height of the giant Goliath is expressed in the Bible as six cubits and a span, the cubit being the length from elbow to finger tip, and the span the distance between the tips of the outstretched thumb and little finger.

The foot was another very early measurement of length; the Roman foot had a length but slightly shorter than our own, and other ancient nations possessed a similar unit of length. Our English foot has varied in length from time to time; the Saxons had a foot of twelve inches as early as 950 A.D., and this was the length of the standard (or model) foot preserved by the English kings at Winchester and removed to Westminster in Norman times. In the fifteenth century thirteen inches was commonly used as a foot length in building.

The division of the foot into twelve inches has come down to us from Roman times, the word 'inch' being derived from a Latin word meaning 'the twelfth part.' An inch is a very convenient small unit of length, for it is practically the width of a person's thumb; a Scottish king in the twelfth century is said to have decreed that an inch was to be the average width of the thumbs of a small man, a large man, and a man of medium size. It is also interesting to recall that the French word 'pouce' means both thumb and inch.

The word 'yard' originally meant a rod or a wand, later it denoted quite a variety of measures of length and area, and finally it has come to represent a length of three feet. The yard, not the foot, is our standard of length at the present time and is the distance between the centres of two gold plugs inserted in a bronze bar which is kept at the Board of Trade. It is supported upon rollers so that it is free to expand or contract with various changes of temperature, but the measurement of the standard yard is always estimated at a temperature of 62° Fahrenheit.

The rod, pole, or perch—that perplexing and inconvenient multiple of the yard—has perhaps been derived from the length of an ox-goad carried by the husbandman during field operations. This unit, after certain variations in length, became fixed at 5½ yards not later than the time of Edward I. It has probably had much influence on the development of other

Imperial measures; for instance a length of 40 rods was a convenient distance for cattle to plough before halting to take breath, and thus the furrow-length or furlong (furrow-long) tended to become 40 rods in length, or the length of the ploughed patch or field.

A rod's distance, again, was probably a sufficient width or space in which the team could be turned round before commencing their return journey, and from this would arise the 'rood,' a unit of area having a length of 40 rods and a width of one rod. Four such roods would make an acre, and 40 would give a square field of ten acres.

Our word 'mile' has arisen from a Roman phrase 'millia passuum,' which meant a thousand paces, each pace being a double step. The old English mile was similarly 1000 paces, or double steps of five feet each. Its length was increased to 5280 feet by a statute of Queen Elizabeth's reign, when it was made to contain eight field furlongs.

A new land measure was introduced by Gunter in the early part of the seventeenth century. This consisted of a chain, four rods in length and divided into 100 equal parts called links. It is widely used by surveyors, and decimalises our larger land measures in a most convenient manner.

Turning now to our Imperial weights, we find that the words 'pound' and 'ounce' are both legacies from the Romans. That ancient nation had a pound weight divisible into twelve ounces of 437 grains each; indeed 'ounce' and 'inch' are both derived from the same Latin word, 'uncia,' which means a twelfth part. This method of reckoning twelve ounces to the pound was long used in England when weighing precious metals, drugs, and bread—i.e. they were weighed in pounds Troy; but along with the Troy pound there was another pound of 16 ounces which was in common use.

This was the averdepois (or less correctly avoirdupois) pound, or the pound used for weighing heavy goods, and it was fixed in Queen Elizabeth's reign at 16 ounces of 437½ grains each. The averdepois pound has remained of this weight until the present time; it is heavier than the Troy pound, which is only 5760 grains in weight. The Imperial standard pound, kept at the Board of Trade, is the weight (in vacuo) of a platinum cylinder about 1⅓ inches in height and a little more than one inch in diameter. When used it is carefully moved by means of an ivory fork which fits into a groove in the side of the weight.

Our English measures of weight tended to run in twos or multiples of two, traces of which remain to-day in the 8 lb. stone of meat and occasionally the 16 lb. stone of cheese. The stone used to be 16 lbs., but was altered to 14 lbs. about the time of Edward III. This monarch also changed the hundredweight (which till that time had been 100 lbs. weight) to 112 lbs.—an awkward weight commercially. The cental or 100 lbs. weight has been recognised as a lawful unit since 1879, and its subdivisions of 50, 20, 10, and 5 lbs. were legalised in 1902. This is a great boon to commercial firms, notably those engaged in the tobacco and grain trades and having dealings with America, where the 100 lbs. weight is in common use.

As in earlier times we had two pounds existing side by side, so also there were two measures of capacity, the corn bushel and the wine bushel, divisible respectively into eight corn and wine gallons. The wine bushel had a capacity of a cubic foot, and the corn bushel was a somewhat larger measure. After much variation in capacity the gallon was decreed in 1824 to contain 277·3 cubic inches or 10 lbs. of pure water measured at 62° F. This is our modern standard of capacity—the Imperial gallon—which is used alike for dry or liquid measure.

The importance of correct standards of our weights and measures is self-evident. At the present day the Standards Department of the Board of Trade possesses authentic specimens of the standard yard, pound, and gallon, these being the originals from which all other copies are derived. In addition to these standards, other perfectly accurate copies or duplicates are kept at the Mint, the Royal Observatory, and several other places. Standards of length are inserted on the outer wall of Greenwich Observatory, and lengths of 100 feet and a chain are marked upon the granite steps in Trafalgar Square in London.

The necessity of having duplicate standards in different places was shown in 1834 when the Houses of Parliament were burnt down, for the standard pound was lost and the standard yard was injured. The oldest existing English standards are those of Henry VII's reign.

Much of the work of making correct copies of the various standards is done at the National Physical Laboratory in Middlesex, and other nations have similar institutions. Our various county and borough councils have control over the weights and measures used in their districts, and employ inspectors for this purpose. Very moderate fees are charged to tradesmen for the verification of their weights and measures, consequently any dishonest person giving short weight or short measure fully deserves the heavy penalties inflicted for this class of fraud.

In conclusion, many trades in the United Kingdom employ special weights and measures, and although we may sometimes find the same name used, its significance may vary according to the particular trade. A barrel

1   2   3   4

Old English Standards

1. *Winchester Bushel of Henry VII ;* 2. *Standard Hundredweight* (112 *lbs.*) *of Elizabeth ;* 3. *Ale Gallon of Henry VII ;* 4. *The old Wine Gallon*

of anchovies contains 30 lbs., of flour 196 lbs., of candles 120 lbs., or of gunpowder 100 lbs. ; a pipe of wine varies in capacity according to the particular kind of wine ; and trusses of straw, new hay or old hay are of different weights. Again cloves and weys are weights used in both the wool and butter trades, but they are of different weights in the two trades.

2. THE METRIC SYSTEM

In addition to our Imperial standards the Board of Trade possesses standard units of the Metric system, which are the metre, kilogram, and litre. The standard metre is the distance measured at a temperature of 0° Centigrade, between two fine lines marked upon a bar of iridio-platinum; the standard kilogram is a cylindrical weight made of the same material, and the standard litre is a cylindrical brass vessel.

When the Metric system was instituted about the year 1800, all its units were based upon the metre or unit of length. This was one ten-millionth of the length of the quadrant of the meridian of longitude passing through Paris; the litre, or unit of capacity, was that of a cube each edge of which was a decimetre or one-tenth of a metre; and the kilogram, or unit of weight, was the weight of a litre of pure water measured at 4° Centigrade.

More accurate measurements of the meridian have been made since 1800, and they have shown that the quadrant does not accurately measure ten million metres. Again, although for ordinary purposes a litre may be reckoned as a cubic decimetre, it is now more accurately defined as the volume occupied by a kilogram of pure water measured at 4° C. Thus the close inter-relationship between the units of length, volume, and mass, as intended by the originators of the system, has not been preserved.

The Metric system is of French origin, it having been designed about the end of the eighteenth century by a committee of French scientists as an ideally perfect system of weights and measures founded upon a scientific basis. It was intended to supersede the older French weights and measures which frequently had different values in the various provinces. Some of these, however, are still in use, although not legally acknowledged, in the more remote parts of the country, for old customs are deeply rooted in the habits of a nation and die hard.

The Metric system possesses the great advantage of being a decimal system; i.e. every higher denomination contains 10 of the next lower denomination. This decimal basis renders the conversion from one denomination to another an easy process, and 'reduction sums' become a mere matter of moving the decimal point a certain number of places to the right or left. Yet under the Metric system it is awkward to obtain one-third or one-fourth of a particular unit, and in this connection the reader may profitably consider our own system (say the yard) from the point of view of subdivision.

Many people have inveighed against our English or Imperial system as being antiquated, inconvenient, and tending to isolate us commercially from other nations. Undoubtedly many advantages would accrue from the compulsory adoption of the Metric system in the United Kingdom, but on the other hand this would render useless many thousands of pounds' worth of machinery in our factories, and we have not as yet been sufficiently prepared as a people for its adoption.

British advocates of the system have striven hard since the year 1854 for its compulsory use in this country. As early as 1864 a bill was passed by Parliament allowing its use, but this measure was repealed when fourteen years had elapsed. After strenuous efforts, the Weights and Measures (Metric System) Act of 1897 again legalised its use, and now the two systems exist in this country side by side, it being permissible to use either.

The Metric system, although most admirable for scientific work, has by no means displaced our older system in trade and in everyday life; and judging by the exceedingly slow progress it has made, it will never do so until laws are passed rendering illegal the use of our own familiar weights and measures.

The slow progress of the system in the United Kingdom is a marked contrast to its rapid spread in other parts of the world. It is obligatory in about 14 European countries and also in the chief countries of Central and South America. On the other hand the United States of America, Japan, Russia, Turkey, and Egypt, like Great Britain, have legalised its use without making it compulsory upon their respective peoples.

Although many countries have adopted the system, they have not all adopted the French names for the various weights and measures; thus the metre is called a 'stab' in Germany and Austria, a 'metro' in Italy and Spain, an 'el' in Holland, and an 'arshin' in Turkey. Similarly the litre is termed a 'kanne' in Germany and Austria, a 'kan' in Holland, and a 'litro' in Italy and Spain.

An international standardising institution, called the International Bureau of Weights and Measures, was established near Paris in 1875, and has for its chief object the supply of standard metres and kilograms to the nations which have adopted the system;

its function among the nations thus resembling that of the Standards Department of our Board of Trade among the county and borough councils of the United Kingdom.

For convenience in comparing the two systems, the reader should remember that a metre is approximately 39 inches, a kilogram $2\frac{1}{4}$ lbs., and a litre $1\frac{3}{4}$ pints.

The weights and measures of our foreign possessions deserve mention: Mauritius and Seychelles have the Metric system, India and other Asiatic possessions have native weights and measures but Imperial standards are also kept at Calcutta, Madras, and Bombay, the Cape of Good Hope has both the long ton of 2240 lbs. and the short ton of 2000 lbs. (i.e. twenty old hundredweights), and Canada also has the short ton. In other respects our possessions have the weights and measures of the Mother Country.

The United States of America have both the long and the short ton. Their gallon and bushel are slightly less·than ours, being descended from the old English gallon and the Winchester bushel. Six United States gallons are equal to five Imperial gallons.

3. ENGLISH COINS AND THEIR HISTORY

Ancient British gold coins have been discovered dating back to 150 B.C.; the earliest of these coins bore no lettering or inscription, but inscribed coins were produced in Britain about the time of Julius Caesar's invasion. The first British gold coin after the Roman occupation was the 'mancus' issued by Offa of Mercia;

it evidently had been copied from some eastern coin, for it bore an Arabic inscription.

A gold penny was issued about the middle of the thirteenth century, but our first regular gold coinage appeared a century later when Edward III issued gold florins, half florins, and quarter florins. The gold florin, which was an imitation of a Florentine coin, was valued at six shillings, but as this value was too high it was replaced by a new coin, the noble, about a year later. This gold noble issued in 1344 contained

Gold noble of Edward III

about as much gold as our modern half-sovereign, but its value was approximately twice as much. It bore the figure of an armed king in a ship and is thought to have commemorated the naval victory of Sluis.

Edward IV's angel noble was copied from a French coin; it appeared in 1470 and bore the figure of St Michael slaying the dragon. Its value varied from 6s. 8d. to 10s. Rose-nobles bearing the rose as an emblem of the Yorkists were also issued in Edward IV's reign.

The guinea was first produced in 1663, and was so

named because it was made of gold brought from the Guinea Coast by the African Company, whose arms it bore. Its value rose until in 1694 it was worth 30*s*., but about twenty years afterwards its value was fixed as at present. The coinage of guineas and fractions of guineas ceased in 1813, and in 1817 the sovereign became our standard gold coin. Spade guineas were issued by George III. The guinea is not now in actual use; it is a coin of account. It is a 'polite' coin, used in stating professional charges and in fixing subscriptions.

The sovereign appeared in 1489 in Henry VII's reign. It took its name from the figure of the King seated on his throne and bearing his royal insignia, and its weight was 240 grains. Henry VII issued sovereigns bearing a double rose signifying the union of the rival houses of Lancaster and York by his marriage with Elizabeth of York. James I called the coin a 'unite' to commemorate the union of England and Scotland. The name sovereign was resumed in 1817 when the gold standard for our coinage was adopted. Half sovereigns were also issued at this time.

Although silver coins had been manufactured in Britain before the time of Offa of Mercia, his silver penny may be regarded as the commencement of our silver coinage. Other old English kingdoms coined silver pence from the eighth to the tenth century, and bishops and archbishops also possessed the right of coining. In Saxon times large payments were usually made by weight—240 pennies or sterlings weighing a pound of silver. From the weight of the Saxon penny arose our Troy weight: 24 grains = 1 pennyweight, 20 pennyweights = 1 ounce, 12 ounces = 1 pound.

Silver pennies were practically the only English coin until the fourteenth century, but their weight and value diminished greatly as time went on, until in Elizabeth's reign the silver penny weighed less than eight grains. Charles II was the last monarch to coin silver pence for circulation. Owing to a lack of small change the silver penny was frequently broken into halves and quarters—a practice which obtained until Edward I coined separate half-pennies and farthings of silver. Such silver coins remained a part of our coinage until the time of Queen Mary.

Our word 'shilling' has been derived from a Saxon word 'scilling,' which most probably meant a cutting or a broken piece from some personal adornment of precious metal. The scilling was estimated at five pennies in Wessex and twenty pennies in Kent. The reader should note that there was no actual Saxon coin called a shilling; it was merely a money of account, like the guinea is to-day.

In 1504 Henry VII coined the first silver shilling—one of the first coins to bear a portrait of the sovereign. It was nearly twice as heavy as our present shilling, which has remained the same weight since the time of Queen Elizabeth. Elizabeth was the first to coin sixpences and threepenny pieces. The milled edge upon the shilling dates from Charles II. Although a sovereign is worth its weight in gold, a shilling and other silver coins are only 'token money'; i.e. their face value is higher than the intrinsic value of the silver they contain.

Some coins, such as the half-crown and the florin, are awkward in that they are similar in size and liable to be confused; others, like the threepenny piece and the old fourpenny piece, not only have this disadvantage but also are small and liable to be lost. The three-penny piece came into general circulation in 1845, about ten years before the groat was finally withdrawn from our currency. Silver florins were first issued about the same time; they were called 'godless' or 'graceless' florins because the words 'Dei Gratia' were omitted from their inscription at first.

Turning now to coins made of baser metal, we find that the Ancient Britons had tin coins, and that bronze coins were in use in the north of England in the ninth century. Copper farthings were introduced by James I, who granted a patent to Lord Harrington to issue them; they were small thin coins of little value and were issued from Tokenhouse Yard in London. They were placed upon a sound basis in Charles II's reign, and halfpence also were issued at this time. This ruler also struck tin farthings with copper centres, and they bore a Latin inscription describing them as servants or aids to the coinage proper.

Strange though it may seem, the copper penny only dates from 1797, when each coin contained an ounce of copper and was heavy and cumbrous. We still speak of 'coppers' although since 1860 they have been made of bronze. Our modern penny only weighs one-third of an ounce. Bronze coins, like those of silver, are merely token money. The comparative scarcity of small coins in earlier times led to tradesmen and corporations issuing small tokens of lead or some other metal. These circulated as coin in the immediate neighbourhood. The practice was declared illegal by Charles II, and no one is nowadays allowed to coin tokens to pass for money under a penalty of £20.

The inscriptions and designs of our coins have varied considerably from time to time, and some references to historical events have already been mentioned. Edward III was the first to place the words 'Dei Gratia' upon them, and the date of minting was added by Edward VI. The union of England and Scotland was commemorated in James I's reign by placing the arms of the two countries upon coins, and Anne placed the arms within the same shield.

Separate Scottish coins ceased to be minted in 1707 when the Act of Union was passed. The Scots shilling was worth an English penny and the Scots pound was worth twenty pence. Scotland also had a bawbee worth a halfpenny and a plack worth one-third of a penny.

4. OTHER MONETARY SYSTEMS

Practically every foreign country of any importance has a decimal system of coinage. France and the United States adopted the principle in the latter part of the eighteenth century, and numerous countries have followed their example. As an illustration of these decimal systems of coinage, we will consider that of France our nearest neighbour.

The unit of her currency is the franc, a silver coin somewhat of the size of our shilling and having a face value of $9\frac{1}{2}d$. There are gold 20 and ten franc pieces, and silver coins of five, two, and one franc values. The franc is divided into 100 centimes, each worth about one-tenth of a penny. Silver 50 and 20 centime pieces are in circulation, and there is a bronze series of ten, five, two, and one centime coins.

A 25 centime piece made of nickel and cut with a polygonal edge was added early in the twentieth century, and has proved very convenient in providing a coin of the value of one quarter of a franc. The weight of a franc was five grammes in 1793, and this

Swiss 20 franc piece

French 2 franc piece

French 20 franc piece

weight was again agreed upon in 1865 when representatives of several European countries met together and decided to adopt its value as the unit for their own countries. The countries forming this Latin Monetary Union were Belgium, France, Italy, and Switzerland;

Greece came into the Union a few years later, and several of the Balkan States have joined it more recently.

The franc is the actual unit for Belgium, France, and Switzerland, but in the other countries of the Union the unit is known by different names, as for example the 'lira' in Italy. All these units, however, have the same value as the franc, and like it are divided into 100 smaller units. The smaller coins are made of bronze or nickel. The Belgian nickel coins are also smaller and perforated in order to distinguish them from the silver coins; nickel being lighter than bronze is a very convenient metal for currency purposes.

Norway, Sweden, and Denmark have formed the Scandinavian Union, and have adopted the krona as their unit; this is worth nearly 1s. 1⅓d. of our money. Gold coins of 20 and 10 kroner, and in the larger peninsula 5 kroner, are in use. The krona is divided into 100 ore, the silver coins being 50, 25, and 10 of these smaller units.

Among the remaining European countries Austria-Hungary has as unit the krone (10d.) of 100 heller, Germany the mark (11¾d.) of 100 pfennige, Holland the florin or gulden (1s. 7¾d.) of 100 cents, Portugal the milreis (4s. 5¼d.) of 1000 reis, Russia the rouble (2s. 1½d.) of 100 kopecks, and Turkey the lira (18s.) of 100 piastres.

German
20 mark piece

The unit in the United States of America is the dollar; its value is about 4s. 1½d., and it is divided into 100 cents. There are gold coins in a series ranging up to ten dollars, silver coins of a dollar and fractions

thereof, and nickel and bronze coins of smaller value.
Paper money is frequent in South America and is subject to fluctuation in value. A common denomination
in South American countries is the peso, which varies
from 1s. 6d. in Chile to 5s. in Colombia.

Japan has the yen (2s. 0½d.), divisible into 100
sen, as its monetary unit, and China the dollar
(about 2s.). Newspapers however quote the value of
the tael—a weight of silver worth about 3s.—for use
in foreign business transactions with China.

The Union of South Africa has the same coinage as
ourselves; so has the Australian Commonwealth, but
the silver and bronze coins are of special design. Other
parts of the Empire have currencies quite distinct
from that of the Mother Land. For example Canada's
coinage greatly resembles that of the United States,
and both American and British gold coins are current;
this is to be expected from the history and geographical
position of the country. Newfoundland has a gold
two dollar piece.

The Indian unit is the silver rupee (1s. 4d.). It is
divided into 16 annas or pence. The anna is a nickel
coin with a scalloped edge, and is worth four pice.
The series of copper coins extends as low as one-third
of a pice. Hong Kong has dollars and cents for its
currency, the dollar being Mexican or British and worth
about 2s. In the Straits Settlements a special dollar
of a higher value is in use.

Various proposals have been made from time to
time as regards the decimalisation of our British
coinage, but none of these has received much support
because of inherent difficulties. One plan suggested
that the coinage should be based upon the farthing

(10 farthings = 1 doit, 10 doits = 1 florin, 10 florins = 1 pound), but a very great disadvantage to this scheme lay in the alteration in value of our British sovereign —a coin accepted all over the world.

Recognising the importance of retaining the sovereign at its present value, another proposal was that the sovereign should be divided as at present into 10 florins, and the florin into 10 and 100 smaller units. This would have necessitated much alteration in our bronze coins. A third scheme suggested a gold crownpiece worth 8s., and divided into 10 tenpenny pieces and into 100 pence. As remarked above no such scheme has received much encouragement in this country, with the result that the United Kingdom, with a few of its colonies and possessions, is the only important country in the world without a decimal coinage.

5. THE ROYAL MINT AND ITS WORK

The Royal Mint, situated on Tower Hill in London, is the factory in which our coins are made. It is called the *Royal* Mint because many years ago the kings alone had the right of minting, and the word 'mint,' as well as the word 'money,' is derived from the name of an old Roman temple where silver coins were made long before the birth of Christ.

It has been estimated that there have been 130 mints in this country at various periods of our history. They numbered fifty in Saxon times and were even more numerous under the Norman kings. In Mary's reign they were all closed with the exception of the mint in London, and this has remained the great seat of our coin manufacture ever since. Temporary mints however were opened in various parts when William III ordered a great reissue of our coinage.

As remarked above, the manufacture of coin was a royal prerogative. Early in the tenth century Athelstan appointed minters or moneyers in all the large towns; these men had charge of the minting in their respective districts and were directly responsible for the weight and quality of the coins they issued. Barbarous punishments were inflicted on them for offences against the coinage, and in Henry I's reign 94 out of 97 moneyers were banished for fraud. Other offenders, such as coiners, clippers, and sweaters of coin, suffered similar severe punishments. Clipping coins was a common offence; it died out when the milled edge was introduced.

The minters were also liable to be called to London to take part in the Trial of the Pyx, i.e. the examination and testing of specimen coins which had been placed in a pyx or casket. This duty is now performed annually by the Goldsmiths' Company. At the trial of the pyx held at the Goldsmiths' Hall in May, 1914, both gold and silver coins were tested. 158 gold coins, of which 127 were sovereigns and 31 half-sovereigns, were weighed separately and were found to vary from the standard by only $\frac{1}{3000}$ oz. on the whole. They were then melted and cast into an ingot or solid block and again satisfied the test. The branch mints also carried out similar tests, and all the results testified to the extreme accuracy of our present day minting methods.

Goldsmiths' Hall: the Grand Staircase

Later in our history the minters became contractors for the manufacture of coin, and special king's officers were responsible for its correctness. In 1850 they were entirely replaced by civil servants, the Chancellor of the Exchequer being now the nominal head of the establishment. Of course the real work of the Mint is controlled by responsible civil servants and skilled chemists.

Gold, silver, copper, tin, and zinc are the metals required for our coins. Most of the gold bullion is bought from the Bank of England, which in turn has purchased it from the importers. The latter may, if they choose, deliver their gold direct to the Mint for coinage, but the usual course is to sell it to the Bank, as by this method they do not have to wait while the gold is being coined.

Pure gold or silver coins are too soft and easily worn away for common use, so they contain a certain amount of copper. Our gold coins contain one-twelfth of their weight of copper, and our silver coins three-fortieths. An ounce of gold alloy yields £3. 17s. 10½d. worth of gold coin, and by an Act of Parliament passed in 1844 the Bank of England is compelled to give £3. 17s. 9d., generally in bank note, for each ounce of gold bullion brought to it. An English sovereign weighs approximately 123¼ grains, but worn light sovereigns are received at their full face value by the Bank of England on behalf of the Mint.

The value of the silver in a shilling is about 5d., for although a Troy pound of silver is coined into 66 shillings, its average price during the years 1908–12 was only 25s. Our bronze coins are composed of an alloy of 95 parts copper, 4 tin, and 1 zinc. Like our silver coins they are merely token money, i.e. they *represent* certain fractions of the value of the gold sovereign.

If a person receives gold in payment, he obtains full value in metal, but not so with copper or silver coins. To remedy this no person can be compelled to accept more than forty shillings' worth of silver, or pence to the value of a shilling, or half-pence and farthings to the value of 6*d*.; in other words silver and bronze are legal tender up to these amounts. Our token coinage is of great use in providing plenty of small change for internal trade, but for foreign trade sovereigns or bars of gold are always used. The manufacture of our token coins is a source of profit to the Mint, and enables it to take back all worn coins at their face value. The average life of a sovereign, half sovereign and a silver coin is respectively 24 years, 15 years, and 50 years. The Bank of England has very accurate and ingenious balances for detecting light coins.

The actual operations in the process of minting are most interesting, and some of the machines used seem almost human in the way they perform their particular duties. The bullion is first weighed and chemically analysed, and during the melting process the requisite amount of other metal is added. The molten alloy is then run into moulds, in which it solidifies into bars; these are next rolled into strips or fillets from which circular blanks or discs are stamped out. Each cutting machine is capable of producing 19,000 discs hourly.

Before being coined, the discs have their edges thickened and are softened, washed, and dried. In the coining machine each blank is placed upon a die, on which is the pattern for one side of the coin. It is then surrounded by a metal collar, which may be plain or milled or lettered according to the coin being made; and finally it is struck by an upper die, which bears the pattern for the other side of the coin. The mint possesses about twenty coining presses, and each is capable of stamping more than a hundred coins per minute.

Automatic balances now receive the coins and reject all those which are not of the correct weight, the satisfactory ones being counted and fed into bags by an ingenious 'telling' or counting machine.

Naturally all the operations at the Mint are conducted with greatest care, and numerous precautions are taken to prevent the loss of any precious metal. All waste metal is returned to the melting pot; some mints reclaim metal from the furnace flues; the crucibles and stirring rods are broken up and metallic particles extracted from them, and the sweepings from the metal floors are also treated.

Our colonial mints are worthy of mention; there are two in India, three in Australia and one in Canada. A close inspection of a colonial gold coin will reveal a tiny letter placed immediately above the date; this is the mint mark and indicates the place of manufacture, e.g. C. = Canada, M. = Melbourne, P. = Perth, and S. = Sydney. The amounts of gold coined at the mints during 1912 were: London £33,000,000, Australia and Canada £9,000,000; the silver amounted to £2,500,000; and the bronze to one-third of a million pounds sterling.

6. THE POST OFFICE AND ITS WORK

The Post Office originated as a letter-carrying agency in the days of Oliver Cromwell, but now its functions are exceedingly varied and it becomes of greater usefulness to the public and the state as each year goes by. Its cost of upkeep to-day is about £24,000,000 annually and yet it shows a yearly profit of about £5,000,000, with receipts increasing approximately at the rate of £1,000,000 a year.

During the eighteenth century the road-borne mails were frequently robbed by highwaymen, an event made of rarer occurrence by the introduction of mail coaches in 1784 and completely abolished by their carriage by railway which was commenced in 1830.

The Postmaster General has the exclusive right of mail letter business and of transmitting messages by telegraph and telephone. Carriers are not allowed to be public letter carriers, and telephone and telegraph facilities are only granted on the understanding that they shall be used for private affairs. The letter-carrying business of the Post Office has increased enormously; in 1912 the number of letters carried reached the almost incredible total of 3186 millions—a number about double that of twenty years ago.

The exceedingly moderate postage charges encourage correspondence. We can to-day send a letter to Australia or New Zealand, or 12,000 miles for a penny, whereas it used to cost 8*d*. to send a letter 50 miles. In the early days of Queen Victoria's reign, Rowland Hill initiated his famous penny post—any inland letter up to ½ oz. in weight being carried for one penny; and since that time many additional concessions and facilities have been granted. Thus in 1871 the penny post was extended to letters weighing 1 oz., and in 1897 to those weighing 4 oz.; whilst a 1 oz. letter can now be conveyed to any British possession, to Egypt, or to the United States of America for one penny.

Further facilities in connection with letters include

The General Post Office

their express delivery by special messengers, their redirection and registration.

Official postcards bearing a halfpenny stamp were first issued in 1870, and reply postcards followed some 12 years later. Not until 1894 were private cards bearing an adhesive stamp permitted to pass through the post. The extended use of the picture postcard has caused a great increase in the number of postcards carried—over 905 million in 1912.

Official postcards are still retailed at the various post offices.

Book post (4 oz. for 1*d*.) was inaugurated in 1855 and the halfpenny post for newspapers and circulars in 1870. Any newspaper may be registered at the General Post Office for transmission at the halfpenny rate on payment of an annual fee of five shillings. Printed matter for abroad is usually charged at the rate of ½*d*. for 2 oz., but there are exceptions to this rate. The Post Office carried more than 1200 million newspapers and book packets in 1912.

The parcels post, originated in 1833 with a maximum weight for parcels of 7 lbs., had that maximum increased to 11 lbs. in 1889. Parcels may be registered and also may be delivered by special messenger, but redirected parcels have to bo paid for a second time.

Adhesive postage stamps have only been in use since 1841. Their values range from ½*d*. to £1, and they are used for other purposes besides postage. Many business firms place their initials upon postage stamps by means of perforations. Such stamps can be easily identified, and perforations of this kind are not considered as defacing the stamp in any way.

Money order business began in the Post Office in 1838. Money orders may be obtained up to £40 in value by payment of fees amounting to a maximum of 10*d*. Postal orders are much more popular than money orders. The general public's familiarity with them, and the fact that they were readily obtainable in every town and for various amounts from sixpence to a guinea, doubtless had great weight in causing the Government to declare them legal tender during the financial stress at the outbreak of the great European War in 1914.

The Post Office Savings Bank instituted in 1861 offers excellent facilities for the working classes to practise thrift, since deposits as low as one shilling can be made. Anyone over seven years of age may become a depositor. In 1914 there were twelve million names on the bank's books and the amount deposited was 180 million pounds.

The local systems of the National Telephone Co. were taken over by the Post Office in 1912, but the main or 'trunk' lines have belonged to it since 1897. A person 'on the 'phone' pays an annual subscription and also 'call fees' in addition. Numerous public call offices exist where local messages can be sent for two-pence. A trunk call is a more expensive matter, and it is much more expensive still to avail oneself of the telephonic communication between the United Kingdom and foreign capitals such as Paris or Brussels. The telephone department of the G.P.O. registered 33 million calls in 1912.

Nearly three times as many telegrams as telephone messages are sent annually. The Postmaster General's telegraphic rights date from 1870. The charge for an inland telegram is a halfpenny a word with a minimum of 6*d.*; but for foreign telegrams the charge ranges from 2½*d.* per word to Norway to 3*s.* 11*d.* per word to Japan. One of the most recent and interesting developments of the Post Office took place in 1909, when all the coast stations for wireless telegraphy were taken over. There are about ten public coast stations, from which it is possible to communicate with some 700 ships at sea. Such messages can reach a ship quite ten hours before she lands; the cost is about 10*d*. a word. Certain railways transmit wireless messages at a cheaper rate to ships sailing in connection with their lines.

Long distance wireless messages require especially powerful stations for their transmission. Suitable stations have been erected at Poldhu in Cornwall and Cape Cod in America. Messages sent from these stations are powerful enough to be picked up by ships 1500 miles distant, but only about 70 ships are capable of receiving these long distance messages. The cost to the sender is about 3*s*. per word.

Enough has been said to show the close relation between the Post Office and the life of the people. This most useful institution also carries on an annuity and life insurance business, issues excise licences and stamps for the National Insurance of the workers, and also pays the old age pensions.

7. OUR FOOD AND ITS SOURCES OF SUPPLY

As a great manufacturing nation we are largely dependent on food brought from our own possessions and from abroad. Down to the latter half of the eighteenth century we used to export wheat, but to-day only about one-fifth of the requisite amount is grown in these islands, the amount imported annually reaching the high average of about 200 lbs. per person. The fertile plains of Northern India send us much wheat, and as the Hindus eat rice as their staple food, practically the whole of the crop is available for export.

Loading grain from an elevator

We receive an even larger amount from Canada where the area under wheat is constantly being increased, particularly in the north and west, for specially selected hardy varieties of grain are being more extensively used. Australia is the third great source of wheat from our own dominions, and each of the three original states—New South Wales, Victoria, and South Australia, has a greater area devoted to wheat culture than we have at home.

As regards foreign supplies, the United States comes easily first, followed by Argentina and Russia. The industrial development of the United States is largely responsible for the decreasing supply from that country. The yield from Argentina is somewhat variable, owing to insect pests and uncertain weather conditions, but that from the Russian 'black lands' and from the Siberian prairies is on the increase. Russia stands first on the list of the world's wheat producing countries, with the United States as a close second.

We are sometimes referred to as a meat-eating nation: certainly our annual meat bill reaches immense proportions, the weight of meat consumed being about 130 lbs. per head; of this about 60 per cent. is produced by our own farmers. About 20 lbs. of beef, mainly chilled or frozen, are imported annually for each person in our islands; the vast supplies from the Argentine and New Zealand come to us in specially constructed cold storage vessels. The meat market is also supplied by large consignments from the United States.

About 12 lbs. of frozen mutton per head are imported annually, principally from New Zealand, the Argentine, and Australia. The importation of foreign beef and mutton has undoubtedly been a boon to the poorer classes, as it has kept the price of meat within reasonable limits. Fresh pork reaches us from Holland, and about 13 lbs. of bacon and ham per person are sent from Denmark, the United States, and other countries, which also supply us with tons of lard every year.

We receive tinned meats from both North and South America, and Uruguay is our great source of meat extracts such as Bovril and Lemco. The Australian and New Zealand colonists are very pleased to find in us a customer for millions of dead rabbits, which of

Freezing mutton, New Zealand

course are frozen in order to keep them wholesome during their long journey through the Tropics. Our near neighbour Belgium formerly sent us fresh rabbits in thousands. The fish from our home fisheries is supplemented by the canned salmon, sardines, and lobsters which come to us from North America, Norway and Portugal.

Every year we import about 9 lbs. of butter and 3 lbs. of margarine per head. About half this imported butter comes from Denmark, especially from the port of Esbjerg. Russian butter travels via the Trans-Siberian railway in cold storage trucks, and cold storage steamers bring large consignments from Australia and New Zealand. Holland is the chief source

Butter-making, New Zealand

of our margarine—a butter substitute which is cheap and wholesome if manufactured from proper materials under approved conditions.

Canadian cheeses form a large proportion of the 5 lbs. of cheese imported annually per person; others are sent from Holland, Italy, and New Zealand. Condensed milk is despatched from Switzerland and

Norway, and about four dozen eggs per head are obtained annually from Denmark, Russia, and other European countries.

Our staple beverage is tea, and Britain and her colonies are reckoned amongst the world's greatest tea drinkers. Six pounds per head are required annually; it is interesting to note that, out of 14 million pounds of tea exported from Calcutta and Chittagong from April to June, 1914, more than 10 million pounds were shipped direct to the United Kingdom. Our supplies of Indian and Ceylon teas are on the increase; those from China are decreasing.

Our coffee and cocoa imports are relatively small, being but ½ lb. and 3½ lbs. per head each year. Tropical Brazil, Central America, and India may be mentioned as important sources of supply. We are not great wine drinkers and only a quart per head is brought into Britain annually. This comes from Europe, from California, and from Cape Colony and Australia. During the early months of 1914 our import of Australian wines increased by more than 100,000 gallons. Beer and whisky are the alcoholic drinks most in demand in the United Kingdom; both require barley for their production, and as much land is devoted to barley culture as to wheat. Russian barley augments the home grown supply and enters our land at Hull and Leith.

Other cereals, as rice, maize, and oats, are not all required for human food. We receive 14 lbs. of rice per head from tropical monsoon countries, maize from the Argentine and the United States, oats from Russia and the Argentine, and rye from Russia and North America.

An Australian vineyard

We import 80 lbs. of sugar per person each year; Germany, Holland, and France send us beet sugar, whilst cane sugar is obtained by us from India, Java, and the West Indies. The fruits we receive from our own possessions and from foreign countries would form an extremely varied list; such a list would include

Drying fruit in Australia

apples from America and Australia, pears from France and California, oranges, apricots, and peaches from Mediterranean countries, California and the West Indies, as well as figs, dates, pineapples, bananas, and other fruits from various parts of the world.

8. THE IMPORTS OF THE UNITED KINGDOM

In the preceding chapter the food we require from abroad was expressed in pounds per person annually, but from this alone the reader would fail to realise the tremendous magnitude of our food traffic inasmuch as 45 million people have to be fed and the value of the food amounts to about £283,000,000 sterling. This huge total is divided amongst the great classes of foods as follows: grain and flour one-fourth, meat one-seventh, butter, cheese, and eggs one-eighth, sugar one-twelfth, fruits one-twentieth, and tea one-twenty-fifth.

Our imports fall naturally into three groups: food, raw materials, and manufactured goods; of these, manufactured goods comprise but one-fourth of the whole, the remaining three-fourths being composed about equally of food and raw materials. These figures illustrate exceedingly well our dependence upon other countries for the food we eat and the raw materials we require for our factories.

The following are the chief imported raw materials in the order of their value: cotton; oil seeds, fats, and gums; wool; wood and timber; rubber; textile materials other than wool and cotton; hides; petroleum; iron ore, scrap iron and steel; other metallic ores; and paper-making materials.

Our great cotton industry developed rapidly after Hargreave's invention of the spinning jenny in 1764; and successive inventions of more complicated machinery, the use of steam, the suitable atmospheric conditions, and the near neighbourhood of coal, iron, and convenient ports of entry have firmly established it in Lancashire and the surrounding district. Three-fourths of the raw cotton required for the millions of British spindles is obtained from the United States, although, owing to her own industrial development, her supply to us tends to decrease. The great cotton manufacturers are therefore endeavouring to promote the growth of cotton in various parts of our overseas dominions. We depend upon Egypt, India, and Brazil to augment the supply of cotton from America.

The value of wool and woollen rags imported is about half that of cotton. The Australian Commonwealth holds premier position in supplying us with wool; New Zealand, Cape of Good Hope, and the Argentine coming next. Far back in our country's history we used to export wool to Flanders, but nowadays our home-grown wool forms but an insignificant fraction of the amount required for the mills of Yorkshire and other districts.

Among other imported textile materials, we obtain much flax from South Russia and Belgium. This is brought to Belfast and Dundee; the latter town also manufactures sacking from the jute sent to us from Bengal. Our silk industry is relatively unimportant.

Oils and oil seeds form a composite group of imports required for lubricating and lighting purposes, and for the manufacture of candles, soap, paints, and other goods. Petroleum comes easily first in importance, and its value is increasing owing to the construction of ships in which oil fuel is used. We obtain about half our oil from the United States and a large amount from Russia also. Much paraffin wax is used in candle making. Linseed oil which reaches

us from India, Argentina and Russia is especially
useful in the manufacture of linoleum.   Other imported
oils include olive oil from the Mediterranean, palm oil
from West Africa, fish oil from Norway, and turpentine
from Northern Europe and America.   We obtain rape
seed from Central Europe and from India, and soya
beans also from the latter country.

Sawing timber with steam-saw, Western Australia

Wood and timber are required for multitudinous
purposes: for building, boxes, furniture, railway
sleepers and so forth.   Common woods such as deal and
pine come from Canada and the Baltic; hard and orna-
mental woods reach us from all quarters of the globe,
e.g. red woods from Australia, teak and ebony from
India, and mahogany and fancy woods from the
American Tropics.

The finest rubber comes from the valley of the river Amazon, and we also receive supplies from Ceylon and south-eastern Asia. The substitution of motor for horse traffic has given a great impetus to rubber growing, with the result that many tea and coffee planters in Ceylon are turning their attention to rubber plantations.

Hides, skins, and tallow are largely obtained from

Skins drying, New South Wales

those countries whence we import meat, and the barks and dyes used in the tanning industry are brought from India, Australia, and the Mediterranean.

We draw upon many countries for metals and metallic ores: upon Spain and Sweden for iron ore, and upon the United States, Australia, and Chile for copper. Our British tin mines are practically exhausted, and consequently our supplies of tin from Malaysia,

Tasmania, Chile, and the Transvaal are exceedingly necessary; for tin is used for coating steel in the tin-plate industry, and in the manufacture of bronze and other alloys.

The main groups of manufactured goods, which comprise one-fourth of our total imports, are iron and steel and manufactures thereof; silk yarns and fabrics; cotton yarns and fabrics; chemicals, dyes, drugs, and colours; leather and its manufactures; wool yarns and fabrics; motor cars, cycles, and carriages; cutlery, hardware, and instruments; paper; machinery; apparel; glass and earthenware.

Both the United States and Germany are great iron-producing nations, and as they also possess coal supplies, their skill in making iron goods and textiles has progressed as our own. The student on reading the above list of imported manufactured goods will doubtless consider their importation unnecessary, inasmuch as we manufacture many of these goods ourselves. He should, however, bear in mind that if a foreign merchant, by reason of cheap labour and materials or by excellence of business organisation, can place upon the *British* market an article which compares favourably in price and quality with the home-made article, he will capture the market. We thus find Austrian chairs, Belgian steel rails, German glass, American lawn-mowers and numerous other foreign goods on sale and in use in our own land.

9. EXPORTS AND FOREIGN MARKETS

Our export trade reached a total of £630,000,000 in the year 1913; only 8 per cent. of this was composed of food and drink, 11 per cent. was raw materials, and more than two-thirds of all our exports were manufactured goods. Our foreign possessions received one-third of our total exports.

The main groups of food exported were grain and flour, including biscuits and cakes; herrings; beer, ale, and spirits; meat; and tobacco. The favourable position of the United Kingdom with respect to America and Western Europe enables her to be a distributer of food to some extent; thus she exports tea to Russia, and Indian rice to the West Indies.

The chief raw materials exported are coal and coke, wool, oil seeds, hides and cotton. The wool is trans-shipped to America and to Western Europe, the palm oil to supply the candle and soap trade of France and Germany, the hides and skins to supply the 'morocco' leather industry of those two countries, the raw cotton to Russia, the tin to the United States for the tin plate industry, and the coffee to Europe and the United States.

Three-fourths of our exported raw materials, however, consist of coal and other fuel. With the exception of the United States, we hold first position as a coal-producing country, Germany producing a little more than half as much as we do. We export coal to the extent of one-fourth of our total production; this is chiefly from the Welsh and Tyne ports. About half our exported coal goes to France, Italy, and

Germany, while Sweden and other European countries and the Argentine Republic are also very good customers. The navies of the world are supplied with smokeless or steam coal from South Wales, and three-quarters of the coal exported by us is of this variety.

As remarked above, our exports consist mainly of manufactured goods, and some of these we have gathered from our possessions and from foreign countries for re-exportation. Our two pre-eminent exports are iron and iron goods and cotton yarn and cotton fabrics.

The export of iron and steel, and goods manufactured from them, amounts to over £50,000,000 sterling. Galvanised and tinned sheets and plates form one-third of this enormous amount; iron and steel tubes and bars, fittings, and rails approximately form another third; and the remainder includes wire goods and ships' plates. Our two best customers for goods of this description are India and Australia, other customers of importance being Japan, South Africa, Argentina, United States, Canada, and Germany.

Forty million pounds' worth of machinery goes abroad yearly; this embraces textile machinery for countries developing their manufactures, agricultural machinery for the increasing cereal production in both hemispheres, and railway locomotives, boilers, and dynamos. Cutlery and hardware generally go from Britain all over the world, the United States receiving a large amount of Sheffield goods in spite of her own production. New ships, railway carriages, cycles, and cars are exported to the value of £20,000,000 annually.

Cotton goods form one-third of our total exports of manufactured goods. Tropical and sub-tropical lands naturally receive most from us. We also send cotton yarns abroad, notably to India and to Germany, to supply the textile manufactures of those countries. We export three times as much cotton and cotton goods as wool and woollen goods.

Temperate lands in both hemispheres, both north and south of the Equator, obtain woollen goods from us. Germany is one of our best customers. France and our great possessions also buy largely of our woollen stuffs. The United States, on the other hand, takes half the linen and jute manufactured in our islands. Our export of silk goods is relatively small and is partly made up of goods we have previously imported from the Continent for shipment to our possessions. We ship very large quantities of wearing apparel to our overseas dominions.

Other important exported goods of British manufacture include harness and saddlery, chemicals, drugs and dyes, earthenware and glass, paper and wood manufactures. An earlier paragraph referred to foreign competition in our home markets; it is equally fierce abroad, for all the foreign manufacturing nations are striving to keep and extend their markets and this competition will become keener in the future. British goods have a world-wide reputation for durability and good workmanship, but complaints have been made as regards their higher price and sometimes their unsuitability. Consuls urge that the British manufacturer should study the requirements of his particular foreign market and should issue all his catalogues and trade literature in the language of the country, using of course the weights, measures, and currency of the country concerned.

Mr Wickes, the Trade Commissioner for the

Dominion of Canada, in his report upon the trade of 1913, urged among others the following points upon British manufacturers:

1. The necessity of a closer study of freights, insurance, and packing.

2. The requirements necessary to obtain preferential treatment.

3. A better knowledge of the terms and credits usually given to Canadian buyers.

4. The selection of suitable agents and representatives, and payment of greater attention to the advice given by these agents.

5. The preparation of catalogues in Canadian currency.

6. Adequate supply of suitable samples.

7. Better knowledge of Canadian geographical conditions.

10. OUR CONSULS AND THEIR WORK IN FOREIGN LANDS

The present time is one of fierce rivalry and keen competition among manufacturing nations for the possession of foreign markets, and the successful trade of our merchants in foreign lands is in a great measure dependent upon information provided by our consuls. These are civil servants who reside abroad in ports and trading centres, and one of their duties is to promote the commercial interests of British subjects. They are appointed by the British Government, and receive, from the country in which they reside, an express permission to perform the duties of their office.

In the Middle Ages the great trading towns of Italy and southern France had consuls or magistrates who had power to settle trade disputes, and by the end of the twelfth century they had established similar agents along the eastern shores of the Mediterranean Sea. French consuls were of great importance in the Near East until the seventeenth century, and not until 1675 were English consuls established in the Ottoman Empire.

The duties of a British consul were performed by ordinary merchants until 1825, at which date the consulate was made a part of the Civil Service and controlled by the Foreign Office. The merchants, whose sole remuneration had been gained from fees, were thus replaced by salaried officials who were not allowed to engage in trade.

A British consul's work at the present time is most important and is also exceedingly varied in character. He assists British · traders at home by making reports to the Government upon the state of the labour market in the place where he is stationed, and upon local conditions and requirements of trade. He supplies information concerning commercial finance and any new laws affecting trade; he is also expected to keep his own country informed concerning any forthcoming trade conferences and any developments in technical education.

By his reports a British merchant is guided as to the qualities, patterns, and quantities of goods required locally, for the consul is on the spot and can gain information first hand. Similarly our great engineering firms may hear through him of intended developments, such as new railways and public works, in good time to secure the contracts for supplying the requisite machinery.

The British consul assists our traders abroad in numerous ways: he gives them the best possible advice in commercial matters, supports their rights and their best interests on every possible occasion, ensures that they obtain justice if they should have to appear in the local court, and endeavours in every way to smooth over any difficulties arising between them and the natives of the country. On the other hand it is his duty to see that British merchants do not evade the local revenue laws by false declarations or otherwise.

Again, from his peculiar position as an educated Englishman residing in a foreign land, he is liable to be called upon to perform the duties of a lawyer and a clergyman: he has power to draw up and attest legal documents, to conduct marriage and burial services, and to advance money towards the erection of churches and hospitals.

As regards our merchant shipping, or mercantile marine as it is called, he may be regarded as the local representative of the Board of Trade, sending to it all the necessary reports of shipping and seamen, and of offences committed on the high seas.

He signs the ship's papers when she enters port, and the ordinary seamen may complain to him if their food has been insufficient in amount or of a poor quality. The consul may also be called the seaman's friend abroad in that he assists shipwrecked or discharged mariners, and he performs this same kind office for passengers and sailors who are stranded in a foreign port.

Some British merchants think that the consuls have too much to do, and that it would be better to have commercial agents whose sole duty would be that of promoting the foreign trade of our country.

11. BANKS AND BANKING

The Jews and the Lombards or Italian merchants were the first bankers in England, but in the sixteenth century their business gradually fell into the hands of the goldsmiths.   The names of some of these goldsmith-bankers are still represented in the banking world. Banks to-day are great money lenders, but the main idea called up in a person's mind when he thinks of a bank is that it is a place where money may be deposited in safety and withdrawn when required. People have confidence in the safety of a bank because the banker himself has much money invested in it.

Now of the money deposited by the public in a bank, some is in the form of current accounts which may be withdrawn on demand, and some is in the form of deposit accounts which can only be withdrawn after a certain notice has been given.   A banker gives interest on deposit accounts but not usually upon current accounts.

All moneys deposited at a bank can be withdrawn in cash or banknotes, but by far the greatest number of withdrawals are made by cheque.   The cheque is really a promise to pay and the fulfilment of the promise can be claimed at the bank directly after the cheque is received.   If the receiver of the cheque takes it to the bank on which it was drawn and cashes it, or if he deposits it with his own banker and the specified sum is placed to his credit in the books of the bank, so far as he is concerned the transaction is complete. Thus no money actually passes between the debtor and creditor, but the result is the same. The power of making payments by cheques is a great convenience to the customers of a bank; it is also a much safer method of payment than by cash.

We have in the preceding paragraph regarded the bank from the customer's point of view, but it must

Facsimile of a cheque

not be forgotten that the banker is a business man whose object is to make a profit for himself. To do this he must trade with his clients' money as well as with his own, always taking care that he has sufficient cash in hand to pay the normal amount of withdrawals, and also sufficient money invested in the Bank of England to safeguard himself if there should be a run upon his bank. In June, 1914, ten of the leading banks had £75,000,000 cash either in hand or invested in the Bank of England.

A banker is perfectly justified in trading with

his customers' money, for by the law of the land it *belongs* to him, subject to his refunding the money when they desire it or honouring their cheques when they are presented. His customers' withdrawals are less than their deposits, hence he has a balance always left with him and the more he trades with their money the greater his own profit will be. His greatest care, however, is to invest in such a way that he can readily obtain the money when it is required.

Part of it he invests in Consols and other safe securities such as railway stocks, but inasmuch as these are *safe* they bring in only a low rate of interest. Another part he may lend to bill-brokers who frequently require money for short periods, and are prepared to repay it either upon demand or upon short notice. This is a more profitable investment for the banker than those mentioned above.

The most profitable part of his business is to advance money to his customers upon their depositing securities with him for the amount. His most usual plan, however, is to allow them to 'overdraw' their accounts, i.e. he lends credit not cash to his customers, and this costs him nothing, but he charges interest just the same. Another profitable source of income is from buying or discounting bills from his customers. Bill-broking and discounting will be dealt with in a later chapter; it will suffice here to state that a banker, in discounting a bill for a client, really purchases a debt due to the latter, and relies upon the commercial stability and good faith of firms that they will meet their liabilities.

The vast fabric of the commercial world is built

upon credit, and in a time of steady trade all goes well; but overtrading and rash speculation sometimes cause a collapse of credit or a panic as it is called. At such times there are 'runs' upon the banks, i.e. customers desire to make withdrawals of *cash*. When a bank cannot stand the strain of such a run, it closes its doors and suspends payment, and on such a stoppage of payment the customers may get only a portion of their money back. During the period of financial stress in August, 1914, the banks of the United Kingdom were closed for several days; this effectually prevented any panic which might have arisen owing to the outbreak of the war, and enabled the bankers and the Government to take concerted action with a view to relieving the scarcity of money.

In London alone there are 150 banks, and there are others in the provinces possessing no London offices. Some are private banks in which each partner has unlimited liability; these however are decreasing in number, owing partly to amalgamation with others. A recent amalgamation was that of Messrs Coutts and Co. and Messrs Robarts, Lubbock and Co., which was arranged in July, 1914. Both these banks were old established concerns, the one dating from 1692 and the other from 1770.

The chief feature of modern banking in the United Kingdom has been the rise of the Joint Stock Banks, which are limited liability companies. Their development into powerful banking institutions is of recent date, for only since 1833 have they been allowed to carry on a deposit business in London.

Although all banks carry on a deposit business, there are relatively few English banks which have the right to issue bank notes—a right possessed by the Scottish and Irish banks. The curtailment of the right of issue does not greatly matter nowadays in view of the great development of the cheque system. The Bank of England is the important bank of issue in this country, and the term 'bank note' is practically the same as 'Bank of England note.' Although many bankers are not allowed to issue notes, their powers of granting credit are in no sense limited, for they can permit cheques to be drawn upon them for an unlimited amount.

12. THE BANK OF ENGLAND

The Bank of England, 'the Old Lady of Thread-needle Street,' was founded in 1694 in order to raise a loan for the Government. It has occupied its present site since 1732, although the original building has been greatly enlarged since that date. Its business has grown enormously, its capital has increased from £1,200,000 to £14,553,000, and its staff from 54 to 1400 persons. Its affairs are controlled by a Governor, Deputy Governor, and a body of 24 Directors. These are elected by the proprietors and include members of financial houses of high repute; English bankers are excluded from the Directorate.

Its origin was due to the Whigs who wished to support William III and to prevent the return of the Stewarts. It was the first joint stock bank having the power of issuing bank notes. From its commencement

The Bank of England and the Royal Exchange

in 1694, in addition to doing much to develop industry
and commerce, the Bank has always been a powerful
friend of the Government. It is the banker for the
Government and does all its financial business: all
revenues are paid into it; it manages the National Debt
and pays the interest upon Government Stock; and in
war time and when large amounts of money are required,
it is entrusted with the raising of the necessary funds.

The Bank's issue of bank notes is a very important
function. It has power to issue £18,500,000 more
than it has gold kept in reserve, but for every note
issued above that amount, it must hold an equivalent
amount of coin or bullion in its coffers. Only upon
three occasions has the Bank received powers of issue
more extended than these. Its notes are legal tender
for any amount and are practically as good as actual
gold coin, for the Bank is compelled to give gold for
notes if required. The notes issued do not long remain
in circulation.

The amounts in circulation do not vary very greatly;
notwithstanding the great expansion of trade during
the last half century, the average value of the notes in
circulation has only increased by about £4,000,000.
The explanation lies in the greatly extended use of
cheques—a device which originated among London
bankers about 1780, soon after their own rights of
note issue had been curtailed.

The design of the bank notes and the paper of
which they are made render forgery a difficult matter.
Until 1914 it was not usual for the Bank to issue notes
of a less face value than £5; at that time, however,
Treasury notes were issued of £1 and 10*s*. face value,
and these, aided by postal orders, which were declared

legal tender, as a temporary expedient, greatly relieved the scarcity of coin.

The Bank of England is a great dealer in bullion or uncoined gold. It pays £3. 17s. 9d. per ounce for bar gold and sends it to the Mint for coinage when required. Those having gold to sell prefer to deal with the Bank rather than deliver their bullion to the Mint and wait for payment until it has been coined. The bullion and gold coin held by the Bank is further increased by the cash balances kept there by bankers in all parts of the kingdom. It holds our central reserve of gold and serves as a bank for other banks.

The Bank of England does not give interest upon its deposits; it is more a national institution than a bank. Nevertheless it engages in the usual banking investment business and earns profits. The rate at which it is willing to lend money is called the 'bank rate,' which varies normally from about $2\frac{1}{2}$ to 5 per cent. and is higher than the rate at which money can be borrowed from other banks. In August, 1914, the bank rate rose to 10 per cent., but was reduced to 5 per cent. within a week's time.

To ensure the greater stability of the Bank of England, the Bank Charter Act of 1844 directed that the Banking and Issue Departments should be kept quite distinct, and also that a weekly statement of the Bank's finances should be published.

The 'bank return,' as it is called, is published in the principal newspapers on each Friday, and gives figures relating to the week ending upon the previous Wednesday. The following is a copy of the bank return published on Friday, September 18th, 1914.

BANK OF ENGLAND

An account pursuant to the Act 7 and 8 Vict., cap. 32, for the week ending on Wednesday, Sept. 16, 1914.

ISSUE DEPARTMENT

Notes Issued . .	£66,484,325	Government Debt .	£11,015,100
		Other Securities . .	7,434,900
		Gold Coin & Bullion	48,034,325
		Silver Bullion . .	—
	£66,484,325		£66,484,325

BANKING DEPARTMENT

Proprietors' Capital	£14,553,000	Govt. Securities .	£25,669,025
Rest	3,755,509	Other Securities .	113,792,525
Public Deposits .	18,643,497	Notes	31,861,597
Other Deposits .	135,042,071	Gold & Silver Coin	686,165
7 Day & other Bills	15,235		
	£172,009,312		£172,009,312

J. G. NAIRNE,
Chief Cashier

Dated, *Sept.* 17, 1914.

This return gives the value of the notes issued by the Issue Department and of the securities held against them; and as regards the Banking Department it states the amounts of the deposits and the way in which these are invested. Thus two important things are secured: the issue of notes never exceeds the legal amount, and the proper reserve of gold is always maintained.

13. THE CLEARING HOUSE

One great feature of trade to-day is that although trade is on the increase, the amount of coin used is not increasing in the same proportion; this is largely the outcome of modern banking conditions.

Let us suppose that there are two merchants, each indebted to the other. In such a case it would be needless to send money in payment of every debt, for such merchants would naturally settle their accounts at stated times, and the one who was indebted at the end of the period would remit a single payment which would close the whole of the transactions. The debts would not be paid individually but would be balanced against other debts.

Now let us consider the customers of a particular bank. They all have moneys deposited in the bank, and when they wish to make a payment they draw a cheque upon the bank in favour of their creditor, who pays it into his account. No money passes, yet the bank's books show that one customer's account has been increased and the other's decreased by the amount of the cheque.

If two persons having trade relations are customers of different banks the matter is a little more complicated, for then the banker at whose bank the cheque has been paid in has a claim for its amount upon the banker on whom the cheque was drawn. But at the end of a day's business the two bankers will most probably have claims against each other, and they will settle these by balancing one set of claims against the other, very similarly to the merchants mentioned above.

There are numerous banks in the country and thousands of cheques are being drawn and presented daily; consequently the balancing of these cheques one against the other is a matter of great magnitude. This work of balancing or of determining the mutual indebtedness of the various banks is largely carried on at the Bankers' Clearing House in Lombard Street. In it bankers' credits are transferred, just as in a single bank customers' credits are transferred.

It is not a State institution but is managed by a committee of bankers. Before it was established bankers' clerks used to be sent to other banks to collect and deliver cheques, and accounts used to be settled daily by bank notes or cheques drawn upon the Bank of England; one bank alone used to keep £150,000 in notes for this purpose.

In 1775 a few City bankers hired a room where their clerks could settle their relative debts, the balances being handed over at the end of the day. The great advantage was that much less cash was required. Some of the principal bankers regarded the innovation with disfavour and did not become members. Joint-Stock Banks were admitted in 1854, and in 1858 country bankers availed themselves of its facilities by sending up daily parcels of cheques to their London agents, who themselves were members.

By this means country cheques were passed on to the London agents of other banks and so reached their destination, without the country banker being compelled, as hitherto, to send small parcels of cheques daily to bankers in various parts of the country. Finally in 1864, the Bank of England became a member of the Clearing House for some of its business.

The great development of the clearing business is exemplified by the rise in average daily clearing from £11,000,000 in 1868 to £50,000,000 in 1912. The clearings for 1912 totalled nearly £16,000,000,000, of which the Town clearing amounted to £13,000,000,000. The heaviest days at the Clearing House are the 4th of each month, when bills fall due, the Consols account days, and the Stock Exchange settling days.

Clerks from the various banks bring their cheques sorted into parcels for each of the other banks which are members of the 'House.' The representatives of each bank then enter up the cheques into their own books and submit the figures to two superintendents who draw up a balance sheet at the end of the day.

Three clearings are made daily, and at its close each bank knows the amount it should receive from, or pay to, each of the other banks. These balances are not paid in coin, but are added to, or deducted from, the account of the particular bank at the Bank of England.

A similar system of clearing has been adopted in our large provincial towns and in some foreign capitals. Banks with numerous branches effect a large amount of internal clearance, and local banks frequently clear among themselves without sending their cheques to London.

The principle of clearing is also well developed upon the Stock Exchange, at the great Railway Clearing House in Euston Square, and among cotton brokers in Liverpool.

14. EXCHANGES AND THE MONEY MARKET

The system of settling debts between persons, especially those in foreign countries, is often referred to as 'exchange,' and is principally effected by means of cheques and bills of exchange. A bill of exchange is a written order to a person to pay a specified sum of money at a particular date to the legal holder of the document.

EXAMPLES OF BILLS OF EXCHANGE.

(i) *An Inland Bill of Exchange.*

LONDON, *July* 17, 1914.

£500

Three months after date pay to Mr A. B. or order the sum of five hundred pounds, value received.

C. D.

To Mr E. F.
   Liverpool.

(ii) *A Foreign Bill of Exchange.*

LONDON, *July* 17, 1914.

£800

At sixty days after sight of this first of exchange (second and third unpaid) pay to the order of Mr A. B. the sum of eight hundred pounds value received, and place the same to account as advised.

C. D.

To Mr E. F.
   Adelaide.

In the above examples Mr C. D. has supplied Mr E. F. with goods, and by way of obtaining payment has drawn upon him the bill of exchange, which duly signed or accepted by Mr E. F. is an obligation for him to pay the debt to any person holding the bill when the time has expired. Bills of exchange are exceedingly convenient, for money can be raised upon them by their sale by one person to another. Bankers and bill discounters do much business in buying or discounting these bills and holding them until they mature; bill brokers on the other hand make their living by buying bills in order to sell them again to merchants and bankers.

Brokers and discounters work largely with borrowed money; other borrowers in the Money Market are the Government, business men, and stock brokers; and the money is borrowed chiefly from the banks, from great insurance companies, and from the Indian Government. There is no fixed place of meeting for dealers in the Money Market; the name implies a whole group of banks and financial houses.

The rate charged for discounting bills is termed the 'market rate'; this is high when money is scarce, and vice versa, but it is always lower than the 'bank rate'— the charge made by the Bank of England for lending money. Borrowers thus only borrow from the Bank as a last resource.

Money is an expensive article to ship to foreign lands, for in addition to freight charges it has to be insured against loss; its shipment however is reduced to a minimum by the use of foreign bills of exchange.

Let us suppose that a merchant *A* in Paris owes

£200 to a merchant *B* in London, and that a merchant *C* in London owes £200 to *D* another merchant in Paris.   If the debts were paid in cash, two sums of money would make an expensive journey across the Channel, but the use of bills renders this unnecessary. *B* in London draws a bill upon *A* in Paris and sells it to *C*: *C* sends this bill to his creditor *D* in Paris, who cashes it by obtaining the money from *A*.

London	London	London
B *C*	*B* *C*	*B* ◄- - - *C*
£200	£200	
————	————	
A *D*	*A* *D*	*A* - - -► *D*
£200	£200	
Paris	Paris	Paris
Fig. 1	Fig. 2	Fig. 3

This may be represented diagrammatically ; *A*, *B*, *C*, *D*, represent the merchants, and the horizontal line the Channel.   Figs. 1 and 2 show the circumstances before and after the operation, whilst the dotted arrows in fig. 3 show the routes taken by the money when bills are used, as contrasted with the double journey across the sea as represented by the firm arrows if coin only were used.

Foreign bill brokers and financiers in London and other great financial centres carry on a lucrative business by buying and selling bills drawn upon other countries.   The prices obtained for bills are not the same as their face values, but depend upon the number of bills available, i.e. upon the relative indebtedness of our own and foreign merchants.   The prices, which are known as the 'rates of exchange,' do not as a rule vary beyond the specie points. The rates of exchange are determined by the foreign brokers, bankers and other financiers who meet at our Royal Exchange for a few hours twice a week, and similar duties are performed by other financiers in foreign commercial centres.

When the demand for foreign bills exceeds the supply, the foreign bankers, etc., in London make good the deficit or 'balance of trade' by drawing bills upon their agents abroad and by paying for these bills with securities or with coin and bullion if absolutely necessary.

A specimen table is given on page 64 of exchange rates prevailing at foreign financial centres for bills and cheques drawn upon London in the middle of July, 1914. The first column gives the foreign city and the class of 'paper money' dealt with: cheques, bills payable at sight or after so many days, and telegraphic transfers upon receipt of which a bank will agree to pay the money.

The second and third columns quote the rates of exchange. For most European countries the commercial equivalents of the sovereign are given in foreign units, e.g. in francs (Paris and Brussels), marks (Germany), kroners (Vienna), gulden (Amsterdam), and lire (Italy). For St Petersburg the number of roubles to £10 is given. In other cases the unit of foreign currency is omitted, but its value in shillings and pence are quoted; as for the milreis (Lisbon), dollar (Hong Kong and Singapore), yen (Yokohama), and paper peso (Valparaiso).

EXCHANGE RATES.

Latest Continental and other exchange rates on London are as under:

	Latest Quotation	Previous Quotation
Paris, cheques	25.16–17	25.16–17
Brussels, cheques	25.28–29	25.28½–29½
Germany, 8 days	20.47	20.46½
Ditto, sight	20.49¼	20.49½
Vienna, sight	24.17½	24.17½
Amsterdam, sight	12.11½	12.11¼
Italy, sight	25.25½–27½	25.26–28
Madrid, sight	26.06–16	26.06–16
Lisbon, sight	$45\frac{15}{16}$–$46\frac{7}{16}d$.	$45\frac{15}{16}$–$46\frac{7}{16}d$.
Copenhagen, sight	18.23½–26½	18.23½–26½
Stockholm, sight	18.22½–25½	18.22½–25½
Switzerland, sight	25.17–18	25.17–18
St Petersburg, 3 m.	95.82–92	95.82–92
Ditto, sight	95.10	95.10
Egypt, sight	$97\frac{5}{8}$	$97\frac{5}{8}$
Bombay, T.T.	1s. $3\frac{5}{8}d$.	1s. $3\frac{11}{32}d$.
Calcutta, T.T.	1s. $3\frac{5}{8}d$.	1s. $3\frac{11}{32}d$.
Hong Kong, T.T.	1s. 10d.	1s. $10\frac{1}{16}d$.
Shanghai, T.T.	2s. $5\frac{3}{8}d$.	2s. $5\frac{1}{4}d$.
Singapore, T.T.	2s. $3\frac{5}{16}d$.	2s. $3\frac{5}{16}d$.
Yokohama, T.T.	2s. $0\frac{3}{8}d$.	2s. $0\frac{3}{8}d$.
Rio de Janeiro, 90 days sight	1s. $4\frac{1}{32}d$.	1s. $4\frac{1}{32}d$.
Valparaiso, 90 days com. paper	$9\frac{21}{32}d$.	$9\frac{21}{32}d$.
Buenos Ayres, 90 days com. paper	$47\frac{11}{16}d$.	$47\frac{11}{16}d$.
Monte Video, 90 days com. paper	$51\frac{3}{32}d$.	$51\frac{3}{32}d$.

15. BULLION AND GOLD RESERVES

When foreign bills of exchange are dear the exchange is said to be unfavourable to us and there is a tendency for gold to leave our country. This is undesirable inasmuch as a relatively small stock of gold held by the Bank of England supports a huge credit business.

Bullion comes to us direct from gold-producing countries; it also tends to be remitted to us when the exchanges are in our favour, when the foreign trade in British goods is brisk, and when the home trade of any foreign country is suddenly diminished.

The outflow of bullion from Great Britain is promoted by our indebtedness to foreign countries, by a decrease in our exports, by foreign markets being overstocked with our goods, and by the failure of our wheat crops.

Gold, like all other commodities, tends to find its way to the dearest market. This is well seen in the transfer of gold from London to continental centres when it is more plentiful here than there. If the discount rate abroad is much higher than in London it pays a foreign broker to draw bills upon his agent abroad, get them discounted here, and ship the proceeds (i.e. gold) to him.

There is thus a drain upon our gold reserves whenever money is very cheap. This is increased by brokers abroad sending their bills here to be discounted, and the only way to check the outflow is by the Bank of England raising the rate of discount. This induces foreign financiers to buy bills here and consequently

gold is kept in the country. Our money market is
exceedingly sensitive, owing to the limited amount of
gold in stock, and commercial crises can only be
averted by the banks retaining as much gold as possible
in their coffers. The Bank of England has been said
to hoard gold, and has been represented in caricature
as an elderly spinster with a stocking full of gold, but
from what has been said in this and previous chapters
the reader will agree that the accumulation of coin
and bullion by the Bank is a very necessary provision
to ensure financial stability in the world of commerce.

The following extracts from the report of a speech
by Sir Felix Schuster in July, 1914, at a meeting of
the Union of London and Smith's Bank is exceedingly
interesting in this connection. He said that during
the last twelve months the Banks of Germany, of
France, and of Russia had increased their stocks of
gold by eleven, thirty, and eighteen millions sterling
respectively. These additions to the foreign gold
reserves were the result of a deliberate policy, and was
it not time that in Britain also some steps should be
taken to strengthen our gold reserves in order to avert
the violent fluctuations in the value of money and the
strain to which our position as the freest market for
gold exposed us? A bankers' committee had for some
time past been considering this question and he hoped
for an early report which might lead to effective
action.

16. THE EXCHANGES OF LONDON

An exchange, in the sense in which it is used in this chapter, is a place where merchants may meet together and transact their business. London merchants used to meet in the streets for this purpose; this was very inconvenient, and in 1565 Gresham proposed to the City aldermen that he would build an exchange or a bourse for the merchants if a site were provided.

This was the origin of the Royal Exchange, which was so named by Queen Elizabeth on the occasion of a visit to Gresham's house near by. Gresham's bourse was a composite building, not only providing 'walks' or rendezvous for the various classes of merchants, but also containing a large number of shops in the upper portion. It was destroyed in the Great Fire of London, and was replaced by a second building, the foundation stone of which was laid by Charles II in 1667. This had shops outside, and in addition to the bourse proper the interior of the building accommodated assurance and seamen's offices, a lecture room, and Lloyd's coffee house. The vaults in the basement were let to bankers and to the East India Company.

This second building was destroyed by fire in the second year of Queen Victoria's reign, and she laid the foundation of the present noble building in 1842. The Royal Exchange has served a very useful purpose in times gone by, but with the growth of London and the vast expansion of her home and overseas trade most of the various groups of merchants have moved to other more convenient quarters. The exchange brokers meet there on Tuesdays and Fridays for an hour or two in order to transact foreign business, and it is also the recognised meeting place for merchants engaged in the chemical and a few other industries. Lloyd's and two great insurance companies have their rooms and offices there, and as will be seen in a later chapter it is the recognised centre for underwriting or marine insurance.

Stock brokers used to frequent the Royal Exchange, but they deserted this rendezvous for the coffee houses. Old Jonathan's coffee house was a favourite meeting place, and when 'New Jonathan's' was built after the destruction of its predecessor by fire in 1748, it was renamed the Stock Exchange. The present-day Stock Exchange in Capel Court is a most exclusive building, and is a great contrast to the old Stock Exchange Coffee House where anyone was admitted on payment of sixpence.

The Stock Exchange is the great market for stocks and shares. The magnitude of its business may be judged by its Official Price List, which quotes more than four thousand kinds of stocks and shares. Its members, who pay heavy fees for the privilege of membership, usually specialise in one particular variety of shares and operate in some special division or market, e.g. the Foreign Market or the Consol Market.

Only members and their registered clerks are admitted into the 'House,' as the Stock Exchange is often called. The members of the London Stock Exchange are either stock brokers or stock jobbers; the latter deal in one particular market and buy and sell shares in the House itself. They do not deal directly with the outside public. The general public give their orders to some stock broker and he transacts their business with the jobbers.

All members of the Stock Exchange must obey strict rules as regards the conduct of their business, for instance they are on no account allowed to advertise. They cease to be members if they cannot meet their obligations to their fellow members or if they become insolvent; in such a case a special official of the Stock Exchange Committee settles all the defaulter's affairs with the other members. The general committee of the Stock Exchange have power to suspend or expel any member found guilty of unprofessional conduct.

Other exchanges in London include those for corn, coal, metals, fur, and wool. The great grain exchanges are the 'Baltic,' a comparatively new building in Leadenhall Street, and the Corn Exchange in Mark Lane. The system of corn factors acting as middlemen between the farmers and the public is said to have arisen from Essex farmers leaving samples with a Whitechapel publican to save them their weekly journey to the Metropolis.

The Coal Exchange, situated quite near the Thames, serves as the meeting place for the large coal factors and the colliery agents. This consists of a central meeting hall with offices around it. As the various colliery agents deal in well-known qualities of coal, no samples are on view. The usual times of meeting are Monday, Wednesday, and Friday afternoons from about 2.30 to 5 o'clock.

The auction room for the fur trade is situated near Southwark Bridge, and furs from all parts of the world are brought here for sale. The fur sales last

for a fortnight, and millions of skins change hands
during that period. The general procedure at these
sales greatly resembles that at the Wool Exchange,
which we will now consider.

We may say with truth that the world's wool comes
to London and that the bulk of it is warehoused at or
near the London Docks previous to being put up for
auction at the wool sale rooms in Coleman Street.

Wool store, Adelaide

The sale of wool by London brokers was originally
transacted at one of the coffee houses; and the Wool
Exchange, which comprises offices let to wool brokers
and others as well as the sale rooms proper, is only
about 35 years old.

No samples of wool are exhibited at the sale rooms.
The buyers, English, French, German and American,

are provided with catalogues, and examine the wool in bulk at the warehouses on the same day as the sale; they don smocks for the occasion—a very necessary precaution in view of their close examination of the wool exposed for their inspection. Needless to say they do not examine every bale, for in one catalogue alone during a recent sale some 8000 bales were described.

The actual sales begin at 4 o'clock in the afternoon, and the sale room is usually filled with buyers, each with his own seat; the auctioneer can thus quickly recognise the successful bidder. This last is an important matter, for the auction is conducted with extreme rapidity, the lots being disposed of at the rate of four per minute.

Over a million bales of wool are sold annually, and each bale contains about three cwt. of wool; it is no unusual thing for 12,000 bales to be sold at one sitting. The first bid made is in pence per pound, the price advancing by farthings and halfpennies. The auctioneers are members of the Wool Brokers Association, a small committee of whom arrange the programme of each series of sales. There are six series of these sales in the year, each lasting for two or three weeks. The brokers receive a commission of a shilling upon each lot of wool sold, and the buyer is pledged to remove all his purchases from the warehouse within a fortnight.

17. THE BOARD OF TRADE

The Board of Trade originated during the Common-wealth, and after an intermittent existence was estab-lished in 1786 as a committee of the Privy Council. Its title of 'Board of Trade' was first recognised officially in 1862. At the present time it is a very important Government department dealing with the registration and winding up of companies, with patents, copyrights, and trade marks, with the conduct of rail-ways, shipping, and trade generally, and with weights and measures.

Its Bankruptcy Department tends to safeguard the public from being victimised by tradesmen who fraudulently go bankrupt, in that it ensures public examinations of insolvents and a just administration of their estates. The Railway Department has ex-tensive powers in connection with railways, tramways, electricity, gas and water schemes, and with patents.

Before any new railway line can be opened to the public, it must pass a most searching examination by the Board's officials, and the public safety is again the care of this Government department when it conducts inquiries into railway accidents. Railway companies are compelled to report accidents to the Board, and since the latter publishes its findings and recommenda-tions in the newspapers the railway companies usually adopt such suggestions in order to regain the confidence of the travelling public. All the bye-laws of a railway company have to be approved by the Board, and it has also been active in securing a greater degree of safety for railway servants.

The Commercial, Labour, and Statistical Department

has the heavy task of preparing returns and statistics dealing with trade, commerce, labour, emigration, and railways. It collects information and supplies it to other Government departments as well as to business firms, and prepares monthly and annual accounts of shipping and navigation. The Board of Trade Journal is published by this department; and amongst its other activities may be mentioned its collection of data concerning the conditions under which the workers live and work, the bringing of employment to the unemployed by means of its labour exchanges, and its beneficent influence in mediating between masters and men in trade disputes.

The Harbour Department protects harbours and channels from injury, keeps a register of British ships, and controls the funds for the upkeep of lighthouses—a duty formerly in the hands of the Trinity House Brethren. Wrecks and their salvage come within its province; it particularly encourages gallantry in saving life at sea, both by awarding medals to the heroes and by helping with funds to reward them.

The Marine Department is another important branch; this department surveys and registers British ships and makes provision for the safety and comfort of both passengers and crew. It enforces proper regulations as to the number of officers necessary in any particular ship, and by granting certificates to officers after examination it ensures that they are thoroughly competent. The officials of this department have power to prevent any unsafe ship from leaving port, and this power is applicable to ships loaded below the Plimsoll mark, or unsafely loaded—as with shifting grain or unventilated coal.

It controls the engagement and discharge of sea-men, and the form of agreement between masters and men must have received the Board's approval. The department has done much to improve the lot of the ordinary seaman by its regulations as regards health, inquiries into the misconduct of officers, and examination of provisions and water when ships are going on very long voyages. Further, the crew's quarters and the provision of lights, signals, boats, and life-saving appliances are all made the subject of inquiry, and special regulations have to be complied with in the case of passenger ships. The drawings and plans of passenger vessels have now to be approved by the Board before the ship is built.

All the money matters of the Board of Trade are dealt with by its Finance Department. This department administers the Merchant Seaman's Fund and the Seaman's Savings Bank. It also provides for the repayment of consuls for the relief of distressed seamen abroad. The accounts of life assurance companies and of those dealing with the estates of bankrupts also lie within the purview of the Finance Department of the Board, and reports upon these subjects have to be submitted to Parliament each year.

18. TRADE MARKS

The Patent Office of the Board of Trade deals with the granting of patents and the registration of trade marks. Trade marks, as for example the familiar bull's head found upon every tin of Colman's mustard,

are symbols attached to goods by a merchant so that
he and his customers can identify them as his product;
by these means the public know they are getting what
they have ordered, for no trader is allowed to use the
registered trade mark of another. It should be noted
that, whereas a patent confers the sole right of manufacturing a particular article, a trade mark does not
do so; for instance, there are many manufacturers of
soap, but the word 'sunlight' is the property of only
one soap company.

The use of trade marks in Britain began to be a
question of importance early in the nineteenth century,
and by 1833 the close copying of any trade mark had
been held to be illegal. Important legislation upon
the subject occurred in 1862, when the Cutlers Company of Sheffield caused the passing of the Merchandise
Marks Act. They were impelled to do this owing to
the unsatisfactory state of the law, which rendered it
possible for inferior foreign cutlery to be brought into
this country and exported as British produce.

Word marks were first included among trade marks
in 1883, and these could embrace 'fancy words'—a
term afterwards altered to 'invented words.' Much
discussion has since taken place as to the exact
significance of this term.

When a person wishes to register a trade mark, he
applies to the local post office for a form of application,
which costs him ten shillings. This form, duly filled
up, is sent to the Comptroller of the Patent Office;
drawings of the proposed trade mark, and a statement
as to the class of goods to which it is intended to be
attached, have to be given upon the form. The trade
mark is advertised in the *Trade Marks Journal*, and

if no person objects within a month to its use the Comptroller registers it and issues a certificate on payment of a fee of £1.

This fee suffices to register the trade mark for a period of fourteen years, after which a further fee is required for each additional fourteen years of registration. If the mark be intended for cotton or metal goods, application must be made to Manchester or Sheffield, where branch registers for cotton and metal marks are kept by the Keeper of the Cotton Marks and the Cutlers' Company respectively.

The object of the Trade Marks Acts is to prevent any man presenting his goods as being those of another, and it is found that fully half the applications for registration are refused. No trade mark can contain the Royal Arms unless the sovereign's permission has been obtained; it must include one or more of the following : the name of the firm represented in a special way, the signature of the applicant or of some predecessor in his business, an invented word or words, a word or words (not geographical) having no direct reference to the quality or character of the goods, and any other distinctive mark.

A trader is not allowed to alter his trade mark in any essential particular, but he may of course withdraw it and have a new one registered. He differs from a patentee in that he cannot grant licences to other people to use his trade mark; he can, however, transfer it to the person who buys the goodwill of his business, for a trade mark is a valuable asset and indeed may be the only 'hall mark' by which the goods are known to the public.

Any person who proves that a trade mark has not

been used for fifteen years can obtain its removal from the register. Trade marks are also removed when their renewal fees have not been paid, when they become separated from the goodwill of a business, or when, as with the word 'linoleum,' they become the general name of the goods.

The Merchandise Marks Act specifies the following as punishable offences: the forging of any trade mark and the manufacture or possession of instruments for that purpose, the application of a false trade mark to goods, and the selling of such goods; but in the last named case the seller is not punished if he can prove that he has acted innocently and has given all information possible as to the person from whom he bought the goods.

In some instances goods are known by trade names, which cannot be registered as trade marks according to the regulations for the latter; the particular 'get up' or method of packing the goods is distinctive in some other instances. It is obvious that in both these cases a manufacturer is entitled to some protection, and the law courts afford him this if he can prove that deliberate copying has been done with intent to defraud.

19. PATENTS

Patents, or Letters Patent, are allied to trade marks in that they afford privileges to particular individuals or firms, but whereas in a trade mark the protection is in respect to some sign attached to the article, the patent applies to the thing itself. A patent is a

document conferring upon the true inventor the sole
right of making, using, or selling his invention for
fourteen years, but it is not usually renewable for
further periods.

Patents or monopolies have existed in our country
for many centuries. Many were granted during the
reigns of Queen Elizabeth and later rulers, and a great
burden was placed upon the people, for many of the
common necessaries of life were monopolies and their
price was quite in the hands of the patentees. The
system was abused to such an extent that James I
was compelled to enact that all grievous monopolies
should cease, and that no further monopoly should be
granted unless it was legal, had no tendency to raise
the price of goods, or had no danger of injuring trade.
The beer, wine, and spirit licences of to-day are descend-
ants of the old monopolies.

The various acts in connection with patents have
been consolidated by the Patents and Designs Act of
1907. A would-be patentee must first forward to the
Comptroller at the Patent Office an application form
which is obtainable at any post office, together with
either a provisional or a complete specification of his
invention. The provisional specification gives few
details, but the complete one—which must be forwarded
within six months of the application—must give every
requisite detail.

If the Comptroller is satisfied he will give a provisional protection to the inventor until the patent is
granted, or 'sealed' as the phrase goes. In former
times patents bore the great seal of the United Kingdom
but now they bear the seal of the Patent Office. The
Comptroller next advertises the acceptance of the

specification and it may be examined by any member of the public. Any person may object to the granting of the patent within two months of the appearance of the advertisement; but should no opposition be made, the invention is registered and the patent granted.

The numbers of successful and unsuccessful applicants are about equal. The fees in connection with patenting an article amount to about £100, and this is a considerable reduction upon the fees formerly in vogue. They are not payable all at once, for this would place difficulties in the way of a poor inventor; there are preliminary fees of about £4, a fee of £5 before the end of the fourth year, and annual fees rising by £1 a year until in the thirteenth year a fee of £14 has to be paid.

As it is incumbent upon the applicant to prove that his article is original—a matter involving much search and technical knowledge, the employment of patent agents is very usual. These can act throughout instead of the actual inventors. They should be men of the strictest integrity inasmuch as they are entrusted, at a time when the inventor is practically helpless, with ideas which may become worth thousands of pounds. The Institute of Patent Agents keeps a register of all agents and examines candidates desiring to enter the profession.

The library of the Patent Office is easy of access and contains the finest collection of technical books and scientific periodicals in the world. It is open to the general public, although it was designed for the use of its officials and for patentees and their agents. Complete specifications of the world's patents are to be found upon its shelves. The Patent Office also publishes an illustrated journal describing inventions, and its register of patents gives all details concerning assignments and licences granted by patentees to others.

A patentee can sell his invention outright, or he can grant licences enabling others to make, use, or sell his article either in some particular district or for a certain period, and he usually obtains a payment or royalty upon every article manufactured under such a licence. All patented articles should bear the year and number of the patent under which they are manufactured.

The Board of Trade can compel licences to be granted, but a much more important point is that all patents obtained in this country by inventors abroad are only granted subject to the manufacture of the article in this country. To safeguard the interests of patentees in various countries the most important states held a Convention in 1902, and resolved that every inventor taking out a patent in one country should be allowed twelve months in which to take out patents in other countries for the same invention. On the outbreak of the European war in 1914 patents held in this country by hostile aliens were held to have lapsed, and British manufacturers were free to produce the goods.

20. LIMITED LIABILITY COMPANIES

Limited liability companies are associations authorised to carry on business by the aid of the capital subscribed by their members, each member being liable for the debts of the company only to the extent of his own share of the capital. There are other companies called Joint Stock Companies, but this chapter deals with the ordinary type of limited company whose members are not less than seven in number.

Early trading companies included the chartered companies such as the East India Company, and the Common Law Companies which at the time of the South Sea Bubble ruined thousands of their members, for at that time each member was liable for *all* the

Somerset House

debts of the company. A great advance was made in 1844 when companies were allowed to be registered and incorporated without going to the great expense of procuring a royal charter or a special Act. This registration was made compulsory in 1862 and the principle of limited liability was established. A greater feeling of security was thus attained, and at the present time there are more than 40,000 limited companies in the United Kingdom.

A limited liability company is usually floated or started by a company promoter, who with six other persons supplies details of the proposed company to the Registrar of Joint Stock Companies at Somerset House and obtains its registration there. A prospectus is then issued to the public inviting them to take up shares in the company, and after the capital has been subscribed a meeting of the shareholders is held. and directors are appointed to carry on the business. The directors submit duly audited balance sheets at each annual meeting and recommend the payment of dividends to the shareholders according to the profits made by the company. If the company proves unsuccessful, it is wound up or liquidated and its name is removed from the register at Somerset House.

The company promoter is one who takes all the necessary steps in the formation of the company. In some cases he is the owner of an existing business which is being converted into a company, but in every case he must make a full disclosure of all material matters and must state the amount of profit he is making in the formation of the company. As the company at this stage is in a state of helplessness, any sharp practice on his part may cripple it at the outset.

The details forwarded to the Registrar are called the 'Memorandum of Association' and the 'Articles of Association.' The former declares the amount of capital proposed and that the shareholders shall have but limited liability; it also states the name, address, and objects of the company. The name must include the word 'limited,' and must be used in all the company's affairs. The objects of the company are stated in very general terms, as they cannot afterwards be altered except at considerable expense.

The Articles of Association set forth the regulations for the management of the company; they give details as to the duties and payment of the directors, the voting powers of the shareholders, and the meetings of the company. They may be altered after registration by a majority of three-quarters of the members, provided that their decision is confirmed at a later meeting. Any member of the public can inspect the Articles of Association of a company by payment of a fee of one shilling at Somerset House.

When application for registration of a company is made, further details concerning it must be given, either by a copy of the prospectus or otherwise, and no shares can be allotted to the public until this has been done. The fees for registration and incorporation vary in accordance with the amount of capital; in the case of large companies they amount to hundreds of pounds.

The prospectus offering shares to the public should give full honest details concerning the company, otherwise a shareholder may demand his money back and the issuer of the false statements is liable to be punished.

The affairs and funds of a limited company are placed in the hands of a Board of Directors. They possess wide powers and should be honest men with a good knowledge of the company's business, especially as they receive and pay sums of money on behalf of the company. The Articles of Association usually provide for the retirement of the directors in rotation, and others are elected at the annual meeting.

Every company is compelled to hold a general meeting of its shareholders annually, and the latter either adopt or reject the recommendations then made by the directors. Shareholders are practically dividend drawers and leave the company's affairs in the hands of the directors; by their power of voting at the general meetings they can, however, influence the policy of the directors. A register of all shareholders must be kept at the registered office of the company, and no change in the address of this registered office must be made without information being given to the Registrar at Somerset House.

The winding up and dissolving of a company is termed its liquidation, and this may be done either voluntarily by the wish of the shareholders or compulsorily by the Court. Fully 90 per cent. are wound up voluntarily, and such winding up usually occurs when a company cannot pay its way. A liquidator is appointed with full powers of carrying on the business temporarily until he can find a purchaser for it, of collecting and realising the assets of the company, and of distributing the proceeds to the various creditors in proportion to their claims.

21. UNDERWRITING

Underwriting or marine insurance takes its name from the insurer writing his name at the foot of the insurance policy. The chief underwriters are members of Lloyd's—an association of ship and insurance brokers, shipowners and merchants, who occupy a suite of rooms at the Royal Exchange.

Lloyd's must be distinguished from Lloyd's Register, which is an association formed in 1843 for the purpose of compiling an accurate register of shipping; this is published annually and gives a list of all ships using our ports, classified according to their construction and the state of the hull and stores. To be A 1 at Lloyd's signifies that a ship is built in the best manner,

Lloyd's: The Casualty Board and Register

is perfectly sound, and that her stores are in excellent condition. Shipowners are anxious that their ships should be placed in this class, for lower rates of insurance are charged, and merchants give such ships the preference.

Lloyd's arose in quite an unpretentious way from

the habit of ship brokers meeting at a coffee house
kept by Edward Lloyd in Tower Street about 1688.
This mercantile community was incorporated by Act
of Parliament in 1771 with the threefold object of
effecting marine insurance, protecting their mutual
interests, and collecting and publishing commercial
intelligence. They have occupied rooms in the Royal
Exchange since 1774, and the form of insurance policy
in use to-day is practically the same as that which was
first printed in 1779.

Newspapers quote daily wrecks and accidents to
ships—news obtained from Lloyd's Casualty List.
Lloyd's are exceptionally well placed to supply this
information, for they possess numerous signal stations
with telegraphic communication—a privilege conferred
by Parliament in 1888. They also publish news
concerning vessels sighted at their various stations.
In accordance with an Act of Parliament passed in
1896, master mariners are compelled to inform Lloyd's
of any derelicts or abandoned vessels seen during their
voyage. The captains of other vessels can thus be
warned of the probable positions of these dangers to
shipping.

Practically every ship and its cargo is insured
against loss or damage, and at Lloyd's the insurance is
effected between the underwriters and the insurance
brokers; the latter are middlemen between the
underwriters and the shipowners and merchants.
The broker offers the underwriter a slip bearing brief
details of the proposed insurance: the name of the
ship, its master, the subject of the insurance, and its
value. If the underwriter accepts the 'risk,' as the
insurance is termed, he signifies his willingness by

initialing the slip and placing against his initials the amount for which he is willing to be liable.

The broker then approaches other underwriters in a similar way, until he has effected the requisite amount of insurance; for it is a usual thing for underwriters to share a risk between them. Sometimes the underwriter gives the broker a covering note or insurance note signifying his willingness, but neither slip nor covering note is the actual insurance policy. The policy proper is more detailed and specifically states the voyage or period that it covers, as well as the risks insured against. It is signed at the foot by all the underwriters concerned, each placing against his name the extent of his liability; thus one document is binding upon the group of underwriters.

No time policy is issued for a longer period than a year, and if the policy issued is a voyage policy it is implicitly understood that the ship will proceed regularly and without delay to the different points of call. Any marked delay or deviation would render the policy void.

Sometimes a merchant desires a 'floating' policy, i.e. one covering goods concerning which he cannot give the exact value or dates of shipment. In policies of this type the class of ship to be employed is specified, and the merchant is expected to furnish the underwriters with true and full particulars as to the value of each shipment as it occurs. Straightforward dealing is imperative in marine insurance, for the underwriters are dependent upon the ship or cargo owners for correct information. The underwriters may cancel the contract if any important facts have been withheld or misrepresented.

The insurance policy states or implies certain 'warranties' on the part of the person desiring insurance; for instance, that the ship shall be seaworthy, her voyage a legitimate one, and that it will be made regularly and expeditiously. Other warranties are expressly stated in the policy and may include conditions respecting the neutrality or nationality of the ship, her date of sailing, and the prohibition of certain classes of cargo. The perils of sea carriage are very numerous and exceed those of land carriage; there is not only the danger of wreck, but also risks arising from collision, fire, war, and other causes.

Losses at sea are frequently referred to as 'average.' In one class of loss called 'general average,' which occurs when some part of the vessel or cargo has to be sacrificed in order to save the remainder, all the persons having interests in the voyage are called upon to contribute towards the expense in proportion to the values of their respective interests. Of course the underwriters have to make such payments good, if the owners have insured against general average. It is only paid when the sacrifice was absolutely necessary.

Particular average is a loss incurred accidentally, as when goods have been damaged by sea-water. The owner (or the underwriter) of the particular goods bears this loss, and others are not called upon to contribute. Losses of this kind are only made good by the underwriters after inspection of the insurance policy and the bills of lading, and the amount the damaged goods are worth is deducted from the payment.

22. THE CUSTOMS AND EXCISE

Much of the revenue required to carry on our public services is obtained from Customs and Excise duties. Customs are duties levied upon certain imported commodities, and customs officers are stationed at every port to collect them.

The control of the customs is vested in a small Board of Commissioners who are assisted by a large staff of civil servants. The duties, as stated above, are for the purpose of raising revenue; they are not imposed with a view to assisting our home merchants against foreign competition. Indeed they are so designed as to place home and foreign merchants on equal terms wherever possible; for example, the customs duties upon alcohol and alcoholic drinks imported into Britain have their counterpart in the excise duties imposed upon the same articles produced in this country.

The word 'customs' arose from such duties being customary among civilised nations. From early times in our history the levying of customs has been recognised as a royal right, and we find Edward I exercising this right upon wool, skins, and leather.

The tariff, or list of articles on which import duty now has to be paid, embraces only about 50 commodities; amongst these are tea, coffee, cocoa, sugar, alcohol and alcoholic drinks, and tobacco. Yet in the early part of the nineteenth century, when our country felt the strain of the European wars, about 1200 articles were subject to duty.

By 1850 the number had been reduced to 150, and

this involved a loss to the Treasury of £5,000,000 annually. The decrease in the number of taxed articles led to a great diminution in smuggling. The customs officers have the right, even now, of searching vessels and persons suspected of smuggling. All persons entering Britain from abroad have to submit their baggage to examination by the customs authorities, and heavy penalties are enforced for breaches of the customs regulations. In 1913 the revenue from customs duties amounted to £33,500,000.

The Custom House

When a vessel enters a port in the United Kingdom the customs officer of the port must be supplied with all details concerning the kinds and quantities of goods brought in; similarly all goods shipped from Britain have to be described in the ship's 'manifest'—a document given to the customs officer by the captain of the vessel when she leaves port. The customs authorities publish daily lists of vessels arriving and leaving our shores; another duty of the customs officials is to make strict inquiry as to the health of all persons upon incoming ships and to see that the quarantine regulations are properly observed.

Imported goods liable to duty may be stored in bonded warehouses under the supervision of the revenue officers until the duty has been paid or until the goods are exported. Before the establishment of these warehouses the duties were paid on entry into this country, and then repaid by a system of 'drawbacks' when the goods were exported. This is an awkward system and only applies nowadays to such commodities as tobacco leaf and coffee berries.

Excise duties differ from customs duties in that they are levied upon goods *produced* in this country. They bring in a large amount of revenue. Duties upon beer and spirits, and indeed our excise system, date from the time of the Commonwealth. They were levied upon all kinds of common articles at the time of the Napoleonic wars, but at the present time they are practically limited to beer, spirits, chicory, coffee mixtures, glucose, saccharin, sweets, and patent medicines.

Excise receipts are further swelled by the licences granted to certain traders, as publicans, brewers, pawnbrokers, and auctioneers, and to private persons for particular privileges. Carriage, motor, dog, gun, and game licences are examples of the latter type, and the proceeds from them go to the various County Councils.

Bonded warehouses are widely used in connection with goods liable to excise duty, the goods being described as 'in bond' whilst they are kept at the warehouses. The establishment of bonded warehouses has proved a great boon to distillers, teablenders and others, for duties are not paid upon the goods until they leave the warehouse for home consumption. When the idea of bonded warehouses was first brought forward by Sir Robert Walpole in 1733 it was exceedingly unpopular and the system was not established till seventy years afterwards. The payment of customs and excise duties before the goods were on sale discouraged both importation and home production. Under the present system of warehousing, the goods 'in bond' may be sold; it being understood that the buyer will pay the duty when the goods are removed.

Many bonded warehouses are in private hands, but the revenue officers have access to all parts, and exercise close supervision over all goods entering or leaving. The keeper of the warehouse gives a bond that he will conduct it in accordance with the customs and excise regulations.

Many processes for the preparation of bonded goods for market are carried out whilst they are in bond; thus alcoholic drinks are mixed, matured, and bottled; tea is blended and packed; and tobacco leaf manufactured into tobacco, cigars, etc. Full allowance is made as regards the payment of duty for loss and waste during these manufacturing processes.

INDEX

Acre 3
Alcoholic drinks 34
Articles of Association 82
Average 88
Averdepois 4

'Baltic,' The 69
Bank notes 54
Bank of England 49, 52
Bank return 55
Bankruptcy 72
Banks 48
Barrel 6
Bawbee 15
Beef 31
Bills of exchange 50, 60
Board of Trade 2, 4, 5, 47, 72
Bonded warehouse 91
Book-post 27
Bullion reserves 65
Bushel 4
Butter 33

Cent 17
Cental 4
Centime 16
Cereals 34
Chain 3
Cheese 33
Cheque 48, 49, 58
Clearing House 57
Clove 6
Coal 42
Coal Exchange 69
Cocoa 34
Consols 50
Consuls 45
Corn Exchange 69
Cotton 37, 43
Cotton marks 76
Credit 51
Cubit 1
Customs 89
Cutlers' Co. 76

Decimal coinage 15–19
Directors 83
Discounting 61
Dollar 17, 18

Eggs 34
Exchange rates 63
Exchanges 67
Excise 91

Farthing 14
Fish 32
Florin 14
Foot 1
Foreign coins 15–18
Foreign competition 41, 44
Franc 15
Fruits 36
Furlong 3

Gallon 4
Gold coins 10–12
Gold reserves 65
Grain 3
Groat 14
Guinea 11, 12
Gunter 3

Harbour 73
Hides 40
Hundredweight 4

Imperial system 1
Inch 2
Insurance 86
Iron 43

Joint Stock Banks 51

Kilogram 7
Krona 17

Legal tender 54
Letter post 25
Limited liability 80

Link 3
Liquidation 84
Litre 7
'Lloyd's 68, 84
Lloyd's Register 85

Machinery 43
'Manifest,' A 90
Manufactures 41
Margarine 33
Mark 17
Meat 31
Metals 40
Metre 7
Metric system 1, 7
Mile 3
Mint 5, 24
Minters 22
Money Market 60
Money orders 27
Monopolies 78
Mutton 31

National Physical Laboratory 5
Noble 11

Oils 38, 39
Ounce 3

Parcel post 27
Patent Office 79
Patents 77
Penny 12
Perch 2
Peso 18
Pfennige 17
Pipe 6
Plimsoll mark 73
Pole 2
Pork 31
Postage stamps 27
Postal orders 27
Post cards 26
Post Office 25
Pound 3

Rabbits 32
Raw materials 37, 42

Rod 2
Rouble 17
Royal Exchange 63, 67, 84
Royal Mint 19
Rubber 40
Rupee 18

Savings Bank 28
Shilling 13
Short ton 10
Silver coins 12–14
Somerset House 81, 82
Sovereign 12
Span 1
Standards 1
Standards Department 2, 5
Stock Exchange 68
Stone 4
Sugar 36

Tariff 89
Tea 34
Telegraphy 28
Telephone 28
Textiles 38
Timber 39
Token money 23
Tokens 14
Trade marks 74
Trafalgar Square 5
Troy pound 4
Troy weight 12
Truss 6

Underwriting 84
Unite 12

Warranty 88
Weights and measures 1
Wheat 29–31
Wireless 28, 29
Wood 39
Wool 38
Wool Exchange 70
Woollens 44

Yard 2
Yen 18

Printed in the United States
By Bookmasters